the MINISTRY of NURTURE

the MINISTRY of NURTURE

a youth worker's guide to discipling teenagers

Duffy Robbins

Youth Specialties

ZondervanPublishingHouse
Grand Rapids, Michigan
A Division of HarperCollinsPublishers

The Ministry of Nurture: A Youth Worker's Guide to Discipling Teenagers
Copyright ©1990 by Youth Specialties, Inc.

Youth Specialties Books, 1224 Greenfield Dr., El Cajon, CA 92021, are published by Zondervan Publishing House, 5300 Patterson Ave. S.E., Grand Rapids, MI 49530.

Library of Congress Cataloging-in-Publication Data

Robbins, Duffy.
    The ministry of nurture : a youth worker's guide to discipling teenagers /
Duffy Robbins.
      p.   cm.
    ISBN 0-310-52581-0
    1. Church work with teenagers. 2. Teenagers—Religious life. I. Title.
BV4447.R63   1990
259'.23—dc20

90-34184
CIP

Unless otherwise indicated, all Scripture quotations are taken from the *Holy Bible: New International Version* (North American Edition). Copyright ©1973, 1978, 1984 by International Bible Society. Used by permission of Zondervan Publishing House.

Edited by Noel Becchetti
Cover design by Michael Kern
Interior design by Mark Rayburn
Typesetting by Leah Perry

Printed in the United States of America

00 01 /DC/ 20 19 18 17 16 15 14

To Steve and Cindy, Mark and Carolyn, Steve and Debbie, Mike and Betsy, Thom and Linda, Frank and Judy, Denita, Delia, Julie, Randy and Sue, Dave and Martha, Martin and Julie, Bob and Pam, Gerry and Joanna, Larry and Barb and the many others who have served faithfully as my volunteer leaders over my years in youth ministry.

Together we have shared the joy and the adventure of a ministry of nurture. Thank you.

Resources from Youth Specialties

Professional Resources

Administration, Publicity, & Fundraising (Ideas Library)
Developing Student Leaders
Equipped to Serve: Volunteer Youth Worker Training Course
Help! I'm a Junior High Youth Worker!
Help! I'm a Small-Group Leader!
Help! I'm a Sunday School Teacher!
Help! I'm a Volunteer Youth Worker!
How to Expand Your Youth Ministry
How to Speak to Youth...and Keep Them Awake at the Same Time
Junior High Ministry (Updated & Expanded)
One Kid at a Time: Reaching Youth through Mentoring
Purpose-Driven Youth Ministry
So *That's* Why I Keep Doing This! 52 Devotional Stories for Youth Workers
A Youth Ministry Crash Course
The Youth Worker's Handbook to Family Ministry

Youth Ministry Programming

Camps, Retreats, Missions, & Service Ideas (Ideas Library)
Compassionate Kids: Practical Ways to Involve Your Students in Mission and Service
Creative Bible Lessons from the Old Testament
Creative Bible Lessons in John: Encounters with Jesus
Creative Bible Lessons in Romans: Faith on Fire!
Creative Bible Lessons on the Life of Christ
Creative Junior High Programs from A to Z, Vol. 1 (A-M)
Creative Junior High Programs from A to Z, Vol. 2 (N-Z)
Creative Meetings, Bible Lessons, & Worship Ideas (Ideas Library)
Crowd Breakers & Mixers (Ideas Library)
Drama, Skits, & Sketches (Ideas Library)
Dramatic Pauses
Facing Your Future: Graduating Youth Group with a Faith That Lasts
Games (Ideas Library)
Games 2 (Ideas Library)
Great Fundraising Ideas for Youth Groups
More Great Fundraising Ideas for Youth Groups
Great Retreats for Youth Groups
Greatest Skits on Earth
Greatest Skits on Earth, Vol. 2
Holiday Ideas (Ideas Library)
Hot Illustrations for Youth Talks
More Hot Illustrations for Youth Talks
Incredible Questionnaires for Youth Ministry
Junior High Game Nights
More Junior High Game Nights
Kickstarters: 101 Ingenious Intros to Just about Any Bible Lesson
Live the Life! Student Evangelism Training Kit
Memory Makers

Play It! Great Games for Groups
Play It Again! More Great Games for Groups
Special Events (Ideas Library)
Spontaneous Melodramas
Super Sketches for Youth Ministry
Teaching the Bible Creatively
Up Close and Personal: How to Build Community in Your Youth Group
What Would Jesus Do? Youth Leader's Kit
Wild Truth Bible Lessons
Wild Truth Bible Lessons 2
Worship Services for Youth Groups

Discussion Starters

Discussion & Lesson Starters (Ideas Library)
Discussion & Lesson Starters 2 (Ideas Library)
4th-6th Grade TalkSheets
Get 'Em Talking
Keep 'Em Talking!
High School TalkSheets
More High School TalkSheets
High School TalkSheets: Psalms and Proverbs
Junior High TalkSheets
More Junior High TalkSheets
Junior High TalkSheets: Psalms and Proverbs
What If...? 450 Thought-Provoking Questions to Get Teenagers Talking, Laughing, and Thinking
Would You Rather...? 465 Provocative Questions to Get Teenagers Talking
Have You Ever...? 450 Intriguing Questions Guaranteed to Get Teenagers Talking

Clip Art

ArtSource Vol. 1—Fantastic Activities
ArtSource Vol. 2—Borders, Symbols, Holidays, and Attention Getters
ArtSource Vol. 3—Sports
ArtSource Vol. 4—Phrases and Verses
ArtSource Vol. 5—Amazing Oddities and Appalling Images
ArtSource Vol. 6—Spiritual Topics
ArtSource Vol. 7—Variety Pack
ArtSource Vol. 8—Stark Raving Clip Art
ArtSource Vols. 1-7 on CD-ROM
ArtSource Vol. 8 & Promo Kit on CD-ROM

Videos

EdgeTV
The Heart of Youth Ministry: A Morning with Mike Yaconelli
Next Time I Fall in Love Video Curriculum
Real Kids, Real Life, Real Faith Video Series
Understanding Your Teenager Video Curriculum

Student Books

Grow For It Journal
Grow For It Journal through the Scriptures
What Would Jesus Do? Spiritual Challenge Journal
Wild Truth Journal for Junior Highers

CONTENTS

DISCLAIMER

Reasonable risk-taking is part of living. Any reasonable risks present in the games and activities suggested in chapter twelve of this book, whether emotional or physical, can be minimized by utilizing safety procedures and providing adequate and qualified supervision.

Duffy Robbins, Youth Specialties, Inc., and the Zondervan Publishing House, cannot and do not assume responsibility or liability for the use of information offered in this book—written or implied.

The bottom line in youth ministry is not how many kids you have coming to your youth group. The bottom line is, "Where will your kids be five to ten years from now?" This wonderful book is about helping kids find and keep a vibrant, active faith in Jesus Christ. When all the peripheral issues and agendas of youth ministry are stripped away, the central reason for youth ministry is helping kids to grow spiritually. *The Minstry of Nurture: How to Build Real-Life Faith Into Your Kids* may be the most important youth-ministry book ever written. It's filled with practical insight on helping kids develop a first-hand faith, and gives the youth worker a comprehensive overview on how to keep teenagers growing in their relationship with God.

If you are looking for instant spirituality, the latest fad or a quick fix, you'll be disappointed. The philosophy of discipleship in this book is the best and most thorough I have ever read. It's biblical, relational, and challenges students to accomplish something bigger than themselves.

The best part about this book is Duffy Robbins. His wisdom, humor and love for kids comes through on every page. Duffy is one of America's finest communicators to students and youth workers. His years of experience in the trenches makes this book practical and insightful. In recent years he has developed the finest college youth ministry major in the nation which brings a depth to this book that, frankly, others have lacked. I admire and respect Duffy's deep biblical faith, his commitment to his own beautiful family, and the joy he brings to the thousands of people he touches with his life.

I know this book will help you

> prepare God's people for works of service, so that the body of Christ may be built up until we all reach unity in the faith and in the knowledge of the Son of God and become mature, attaining to the whole measure of the fullness of Christ (Ephesians 4:12, 13).

Jim Burns
President, National Institute of Youth Ministry

I once knew a guy who was discipling a new Christian. It wasn't easy, and some people must have wondered why he was putting up with all the hassles, why he would choose to look beyond this baby Christian's inconsistencies and uncertainties and bother to pour his life into one young man who showed so little promise.

Sometimes it must have been frustrating to deal with this young Christian's immaturities—like the time he had to be separated from his girlfriend on the bus because they were making out. Or the time he had to be moved out of a hotel room on a mission trip because he kept spitting over the wall at the guy in the room next door. Or the time he had to be threatened with missing a work trip because he hadn't passed a Scripture memory requirement.

The story goes on and on; there were some encouraging chapters, but there were plenty of discouraging ones as well. My friend must have wondered if all of those little hassles, late nights, and long conversations would ever pay off. Well, they did—I know, because that young man was me, nineteen years ago.

Much has changed in nineteen years: the girl that I kissed on the bus is now my wife, I've almost completely curtailed my spitting in hotel rooms, and through the years I've worked hard to build into my youth groups and into my two daughters the discipline of Scripture memory.

FROM ME TO YOU

You're reading this book because you're a rare animal. You're one of those who, despite all the headlines and hype, still believe it's possible to help teenagers have a closer walk with Jesus. The average pastor, parent, high school employee, and church janitor think you're a little strange (okay, maybe a lot strange).

Like most of the world, they're convinced that adolescent spirituality is a contradiction in terms. Linguists call this an oxymoron—

two words that seemingly don't belong together. The comedian Pat Paulsen gives us examples like freezer burn, jumbo shrimp, and military intelligence. Having been active in local church youth ministry for the last fifteen years, I have come up with a few oxymorons of my own: United Methodist (Presbyterians, etc.), Christian organization, and youth retreat.

But like you, I'm convinced that adolescent spirituality is a possibility, not just because this is a youth ministry book and, as its author, I must espouse the party line (laid down by orthodoxymorons).

I'm convinced that adolescent spirituality is a reality because over the years I have seen it fleshed out in the lives of hundreds of teenagers, some of whom in the early going seemed so devoid of potential that I would have predicted they would attain all of the Christian devotion of Darth Vader. Even more so, I'm convinced because I have seen how far a merciful and loving God has brought me from those early days as a seventeen-year-old new believer.

In short, I know the impact that people like you can have on the lives of teenagers. I've seen God take fifteen-year-olds and place someone like you in their lives, someone who dreams big dreams for them, who looks beyond adult skepticism and cynicism and trusts a mighty God to work in the life of an adolescent. And God is pleased to make those dreams a reality. God can use you to help teenagers grow spiritually. This book was written to assist you with your ministry.

SECTION ONE

ADOLESCENT SPIRITUALITY

CHAPTER ONE
DEFINING THE TARGET

The goal of youth ministry is to help teenagers grow spiritually. If we don't understand that at the outset, you can bet that we will eventually find our efforts upset. The church is littered with wasted programs, sermons, Bible studies, and projects which once seemed like wonderful ideas, but were never motivated and fueled by a sense of target. Over and over, people have walked away from the church, not nodding their heads and saying, "Bullseye," but shaking their heads and shouting, "Bull!"

What do we actually mean by spiritual growth? What *is* spiritual maturity? Consider the following case studies:

Case Study One: Recently, Cliff's brother was killed in a car accident. The accident really shook Cliff into thinking about his faith. You haven't seen Cliff at church or in youth group for several weeks now.

When you ask him why, he says it's because he's confused about God, tired of people always giving him the right spiritual answer, fed-up with Christians playing church, and irked by all the games the youth group plays. Cliff wonders how Christians can be living by faith when they don't seem to know what faith really is.

What do these changes mean in Cliff's walk with Christ? Is this some kind of spiritual nosedive? Is this just a normal stage of adolescence? Is this a time of stagnation in Cliff's spiritual development, or is it just a different and more awkward stage of growth? Can Cliff experience this kind of struggling and questioning and still be experiencing spiritual growth?

Case Study Two: All through junior high, Debbie was active in the youth group. She was an enthusiastic participant, attending virtually every weekly event and most retreats. On two or three occasions, she even gave her testimony and took part in youth-led worship services.

Everything looked great. But now, as a junior in high school, Debbie has found that other activities have really cut into youth-group time. She is less involved with youth-group activities and her attendance at Bible studies is less frequent.

On a recent occasion, when you asked her how things were going she abruptly responded, "Everything is fine. Don't worry. I'm still a Christian." But somehow, you don't feel reassured.

Maybe we can explain Cliff's problem as a temporary set-back, unfortunate, but certainly understandable in light of the circumstances. But how do we explain what is happening in the life of Debbie? Everything seemed so promising in her earlier years. All of the "right" signs were in place. Then, just when she might have been expected to blast into a wider spiritual orbit, it looks instead as if she's decided to jettison her Christian identity.

Again, the same questions haunt us. Is this a default on Debbie's spiritual commitment, or a delay in it, or is it just one of the tough stages of growth that she has to go through to get on track? What do you talk about with Debbie during these times? Trials, perseverance, or judgment? Are there any evidences of spiritual growth in Debbie's life, or is there only spiritual decay?

Anyone who has spent much time around teenagers knows that Cliff and Debbie are not unique. There are thousands of stories like theirs. Over the years researchers have confirmed what we have observed for ourselves: Roughly, only fifty percent of the teenagers in the United States who describe themselves as Christians will be sitting in a church somewhere this Sunday. Just two years from now, about seventy percent of those students will have graduated from high school, graduated from the youth program, and graduated from God. And most will never come back.

This book is about turning that trend around. It's about building staying power and maturity into the spiritual lives of the adolescents with whom we work. From all appearances, Cliff and Debbie had experienced some sort of spiritual birth—they had made some initial commitment of faith. But like so many of the students with whom we work, what they seem to lack is spiritual growth.

A WORKING DEFINITION OF ADOLESCENT SPIRITUALITY

In 1987, Charles Shelton, a Catholic educator with a concern for youth ministry in the local parish, wrote a book entitled *Adolescent Spirituality: Pastoral Ministry for High School and College Youth* (Loyola University Press, 1983). In that book, Shelton defines adolescent spirituality in terms of four dynamics: (1) it is Christ-centered; (2) it is experienced in the context of community; (3) it is future-oriented in that it affects hopes, plans, and attitudes about life yet to be lived; and (4) it is developmental. It is shaped and influenced by the diverse intellectual, physical, and social changes that are a normal part of adolescence.

While I applaud Dr. Shelton's thoughtful insights, I would like to suggest a slightly different framework with which we can build a good working definition of spiritual growth. It comes from the ageless vision of the Apostle Paul as he writes to the church in Ephesus.

It was he who gave some to be apostles, some to be prophets, some to be evangelists, and some to be pastors and teachers, to prepare God's people for works of service, so that the body of Christ may be built up until we all reach unity in the faith and in the knowledge of the Son of God and become mature, attaining to the whole measure of the fullness of Christ. Then we will no longer be infants, tossed back and forth by the waves, and blown here and there by every wind of teaching and by the cunning and craftiness of men in their deceitful scheming. Instead, speaking the truth in love, we will in all things grow up into him who is the Head, that is, Christ. From him the whole body, joined and held together by every supporting ligament, grows and builds itself up in love, as each part does its work (Ephesians 4:11–16).

Paul gives us in this passage four key phrases we need to consider to develop a working definition of spiritual growth. Each of the four phrases is critical. Just as a four-legged table needs to have four legs of equal proportion to be suitable for serving the family meal, so it is with our definition of spiritual nurture. Neglect in any one area leads to an imbalance and eventually to an unhealthy, unbiblical picture of what spiritual growth actually is according to Scripture.

The four key phrases are:

1. *"We will in all things grow up into him who is the Head, that is, Christ"* (Ephesians 4:15b).

If spiritual growth doesn't mean anything else, it surely means that students should grow in their personal, day-to-day relationship with Jesus, and that we should be helping them to do this. That almost seems so self-evident that it's absurd to write it down. But, sadly, the real absurdity is the number of youth ministries who still tiptoe around the issue of Christ and his Lordship as if there are other areas of spiritual maturity more important.

The number one goal of spiritual growth is not tithing, church membership, voter registration, T-shirt (light bulb, candy, spaghetti, cookie, Christmas card, glow-in-the-dark posters of the pastor) sales, political mobilization, retreat attendance, or denominational involvement. Rather, the goal is helping kids grow in their relationship with the living Christ. One of the reasons that the Cliffs and the Debbies in our youth groups seem to lose interest spiritually is that we often do a better job of nurturing their commitment to the youth group than we do of nurturing their commitment to the Lord.

Usually this is unintentional. It begins with our encouraging students to come to youth group as junior highers. And in those junior high years before they get their driver's license, we remind them how much fun youth group is, and how critical it is that they have weekly fellowship with Christian friends. We do that at least partly because we know it's true, and partly because we want them to keep coming back to youth group.

I can remember one occasion as a youth minister in Rhode Island, when I had the pleasure of having a student approach me and say with complete sincerity, "You know, I haven't been in youth group the last five weeks and I have got to be honest that in that time my spiritual life has just gone right down the tubes!" And deep down inside, there was a part of me going, "You bet it has, kid. And don't you forget it. You better never miss a week with this youth group again!"

Of course, what we're actually saying when we feel that way is: "You better believe your spiritual life tubed out when you missed youth group these last five weeks, because without this youth group, all you have . . . is . . . God"(!) We tend to forget that within a few years, they *won't* have the youth group. All they *will* have is God.

It's almost as if we've forgotten that our main purpose in youth ministry is to help students begin that pilgrimage of growth through which they become progressively dependent on God—nothing less than that. If we are building students whose faith is dependent primarily on a weekly skit, a creative Bible study, and a summer camp, we are building Christians that simply are not going to last beyond the high-school years.

We need to realize that the task of helping students grow spiritually begins when we encourage those in early adolescence to be loyal and committed to some Christian group, a group they will need as they sort out and think about their own Christianity.

But then the process moves in the other direction. Our task becomes more of a weaning process in which we refocus our efforts on helping the students to individualize their own faith. We help them to develop and sort out their own beliefs so that they can be dependent on God and *independent of the youth group*. I have a friend who often reminds youth workers that this weaning process is difficult, both for the wean-er and the wean-ee.

But that task is vital, because there will come a point at which these students move into their middle-to-late-adolescent years, when they get their own driver's licenses and are less dependent on the church or the youth group for social needs. That's when we begin to find that all of the activities that were so much fun and so important for these students when they were in junior high just don't elicit the same kind of response anymore. We discover that these high schoolers face needs and challenges that a great night with water balloons and eggs in the armpit just can't cover . . . but Jesus can.

That is why our primary responsibility in spiritual nurture is to help students grow "in all things . . . into him who is the Head, that is,

Christ" (Ephesians 4:15b). *Spiritual growth involves a deepening sense of what it means to live daily in relationship with the Lord.*

2. *"To prepare God's people for works of service"* (Ephesians 4:12).

Now some of you are reading that last line and thinking, "But the kids in my youth group don't act very much like God's people; they're not saints, they're *ain'ts*. And they don't seem to be the least bit interested in work, let alone service." But the fact is that God has called all Christians to do the work of ministry. That's as true for teenage Christians as it is for older Christians.

Unfortunately our general unwillingness to call students to a commitment of ministry, to accomplish something bigger than themselves, lives right up to the low expectations that students generally have for themselves. We don't challenge them to attempt very much because we don't expect that they will be willing to accept the challenge. Students often are reluctant to accept the challenge because they assume they will be incapable.

I remember one ninth-grade girl in our youth group who seemed so quiet and shy that I really couldn't see her in any kind of leadership role. Due in part to my own insecurity, I didn't dare trust her to lead a small group for our youth program. Her own poor self-image and low profile in the youth group were very likely a reflection of my unwillingness to give her a shot at a leadership position. I just didn't think she had the stuff.

I finally worked up the nerve to give her a try. To my absolute surprise and bewilderment, she was incredible. Kids actually began requesting her as a small group leader. Her personality blossomed. The group discovered her, and she continued as a strong student leader throughout her high-school years.

Through these kinds of experiences I have discovered that the only way to convince either the students or the leaders that their estimates of their own abilities are too low is by enlisting them in a challenge to accomplish something bigger than themselves. Eastern College professor of sociology, Anthony Campolo, has had a world-wide impact because he has dared to challenge Christian youth around the world to be used by God to change the world. His message through the years has been consistently challenging and penetratingly clear: "You can make a difference."

Within the last three months I have met students from four different states and two different countries who have told me of their plans to work through the Eastern College MBA in Economic Development and go back to their home state or home country and make a difference for Christ. One year ago, by their own testimony, none of these six students had any such vision. But each of them came to Eastern College, whether from California, Indonesia, or New Jersey, because Campolo challenged them to change their world by the power of Christ.

Campolo is effective because he taps into that wonderful part of adolescence that wants to believe that the world can be made a better place, and that one's dreams and hopes can make change possible. It has been the call that has mobilized students in growing numbers over the last century to give themselves to the world mission movement. It is no less a challenge than the one issued by the elder Apostle Paul when he wrote to the young man Timothy, "Don't let anyone look down on you because you are young, but set an example for the believers in speech, in life, in love, in faith and in purity" (1 Timothy 4:12).

People who are committed to the Christian nurture of teenagers must begin to regain this understanding of the call of God—that it is a call to ministry. Any definition of spiritual growth which does not include some progressive understanding that God has called each of us to a life of ministry in some shape or fashion is a definition of spiritual growth that is foreign to the clear teaching of Scripture. We must be clear on this: *Spiritual growth means a growing sense of being called to serve.*

3. *"We will no longer be infants"* (Ephesians 4:14).

It's no secret in youth ministry that we are working with people who are moving through a time of transition. In working with teenagers, we are ministering with human beings who are coping with intense emotional feelings, dramatic physical changes, and turbulent social pressures.

Part of this is pure biology. As we move into puberty and the hormones kick in, we change from thinking that the opposite sex has cooties to thinking that cooties are tremendously intriguing.

Part of the shift is social. Moving into the teen years means that for better or for worse young people find themselves in social settings in which they are expected to be moving away from the family as the primary source of relationships and intimacy. They move more toward peer relationships. There is a sense in which this movement is healthy, but it can also be very difficult.

When I talk with parents and kids about the process of establishing one's own identity and moving away from the family as the major source of security, I liken it to hiking up a steep mountain trail. All the way up the trail, walking companions encourage each other by saying how great it will be when they finally arrive at the top. Sore muscles can be relaxed and the view will offer a whole new perspective. And of course, that's true.

But what we tend to forget is that once the crest has been reached, the trail offers a new challenge, this one downhill. The perspective is quite different, and the muscles that were taxed in the long climb up are not as necessary. The sad fact is that the downward trek requires flexing a whole new set of muscles. While the climb up the trail involved the continual challenge of pushing forward, the descent involves the challenge of slowing one's forward motion enough to avoid the danger of falling.

My own observation is that the sociological and interrelational changes of moving into puberty are very close to this uphill/downhill trek. All through childhood kids are told to move forward, grow up, see how big you can be, act like an adult. And there is the sense in which as a little child we dream how neat and easy it will be some day when we are grown up—how different the world will look from up there.

Unfortunately, with the movement into adolescence, the perspective changes, and so does the challenge. Whereas the gravitational pull on a pre-adolescent child is in the direction of dependence, the strong pull of adolescence is in the other direction. All of a sudden the teenager begins to hear people saying things like, "Whoa, hold on there . . . just who do you think you are?" and, "I'm not sure you're ready to make those kinds of decisions" and "Who do you think you are—an adult?" And—surprise—the new direction of growth and independence requires a whole new set of muscles to prevent a fall.

One familiar window into this kind of scenario is the one that opens onto a car full of children with the mother complaining, "I'll be glad when you get your own driver's license and can drive yourself around. I've got more to do than be your chauffeur." Then we look through the same window a few years down the road, and the mother is saying, "Why do you always feel you must have the car to yourself? Your father and I can take you and your friends to the movies. I just don't feel like you're ready to drive your friends around town without your father or me along."

To make matters even more interesting, growth in the teenage years involves changes in intellectual abilities and thinking patterns, changes that deeply and profoundly impact the ways that we think about God and the world around us. Paul writes, "Then we will no longer be infants, tossed back and forth by the waves, and blown here and there by every wind of teaching and by the cunning and craftiness of men in their deceitful scheming" (Ephesians 4:14). As we work through our understanding of spiritual growth, we are given here two key insights from the pen of the Apostle.

One element of spiritual growth is the important task of helping students come to an adult or mature understanding of their faith. Paul alludes to this transition in thinking when he writes in 1 Corinthians 13:11, "When I was a child, I talked like a child, I thought like a child, I reasoned like a child. When I became a man, I put childish ways behind me." What Paul seems to be saying is that spiritual maturity involves giving up a childish faith that believes in easy answers, and holding tightly to a childlike faith that trusts the Father even when there don't seem to be any answers. Cliff's story of stalemate might have been different if he had faced his brother's death with that kind of faith.

There are some who would interpret this to mean that an adult faith moves us beyond the need for a naive faith that accepts the Bible as true, that an adult faith has the sophistication to recognize that much of the miraculous and supernatural in the Scripture is not so much true as it is designed to point us to more basic truths. That is not at all what I think Paul means.

Putting away childish reasoning does not involve throwing out the babies (biblical miracles, the virgin birth, the sense of a real and active God) with the bath water (a God who helps those who help themselves, a God who always promises physical health and well-being to his people, or some kind of name-it-and-claim-it God). What it does mean, for example, is that we help the students in our youth group come to grips with the fact that even though God is good and loving, we are not guaranteed safety from all unpleasant experiences of life, whether it is a brother who dies in a car wreck, a father who loses his job, or a mom and dad who decide to get a divorce.

That may have been part of Cliff's problem. There was just no room in his childish understanding of God for the kind of crisis brought on by his brother's death. That immature kind of faith is usually adequate for the early years of childhood. But, as teenagers grow into late adolescence, reality is not very kind to those childish pictures of God and the world.

Spiritual maturity comes not with some kind of childish naïvete that is "tossed back and forth by the waves, and blown here and there by every wind of teaching" (Ephesians 4:14), but with a faith that is tough enough to stay afloat even in the midst of the storms and the waves of real life with real questions. It is not explaining away the wonder and the mystery of God; it is recognizing that when all of the doctrines have been learned, and all of the verses are memorized, and all of the basic questions are answered, a mature faith will embrace the dilemmas and the mysteries as matters best left in the hands of a sovereign God.

Paul puts his finger on an additional concern of spiritual growth in Ephesians 4:14b. He writes that spiritual immaturity is characterized by a gullibility that causes one to be easily tricked by "craftiness in deceitful wiles." To put it another way, teenagers are easily victimized by that which looks true and sounds true, but is not true. An important facet of spiritual growth is gaining the ability to discern between that which is true and that which is false.

This is particularly critical for teenagers because the adolescent years are full of important choices to be made from a myriad of options. And teenagers are easily fooled. A television ad campaign portrays a group of guys sitting around a campfire in the midst of pristine northern Minnesota wilderness. The moon is beautiful. The flames lick at the friendly darkness of the north woods. Laughter. Good times. Friends around the campfire.

Then somebody says, "Y'know guys, it just doesn't get any better than this." It sounds good. It looks good. What normal adolescent wouldn't buy into the implied logic: good friends = good times = several six-packs of booze?

Unfortunately, while there may be some truth to this picture, critical thought, discernment, and cold, hard experience teach that it is not the complete picture. The complete picture might begin with the same background, the same beautiful scenario, the same golden flames reaching into the nighttime sky. But this time as the camera moves closer, we begin to see a quite different picture. This time the eye of the camera opens on a scene of death and destruction, four bodies bleeding on the pavement, a smoking car wrapped around a tree, and spilling in the grass along the road, several broken six-packs of beer. This time, a voice more sober and haunting says, "Y'know, it just doesn't get any better than this."

Spiritual growth means teenagers will be no longer children in the way they view the world around them and their life decisions. This growth can be helped along if teenagers are armed with a grid of biblical truth and Christian teaching through which they can sift the propaganda and deceitful strategies of the culture to make wise decisions about their lives.

Adolescence, along with all of the other challenges and changes, brings with it important developments in intellectual growth. *Any definition of spiritual growth in the life of teenagers must involve a movement toward mature thinking about God and life choices.*

4. *"From him the whole body, joined and held together by every supporting ligament, grows and builds itself up in love, as each part does its work"* (Ephesians 4:15b).

During the teenage years, relationships are all-important. Research has shown convincingly that relationships with close friends, whether of the same or opposite sex, are the greatest source of satisfaction for teenagers. This is true whether the survey includes churched teenagers, unchurched teenagers, Christian teenagers, or non-Christian teenagers.

Paul writes that we can't really understand Christian growth and maturity if we do not understand that the Christian life is lived within the context of relationships. I personally believe that there are certain pleasures in life which may be best appreciated as solitary pleasures: cross-country skiing on a deserted mountain meadow, great music enjoyed through high quality headphones, a long, hot bath. But, the Christian life is not a solitary adventure. The New Testament Christianity involves genuine community—not just sardines packed in the same can, but people "joined and held together" (Ephesians 4:16) through a process of "speaking the truth in love" (Ephesians 4:15).

If we expect to impact the lives of young people like Debbie, we will have to help her develop a sense that the other students in the youth group are her Christian community. One of the best ways to help people like Debbie grow spiritually is to involve her in with peers who are growing spiritually. If we neglect this element of spiritual growth, we are ignoring the extreme importance of peer influence in the lives of teenagers.

The emphasis on Christian community is not only a matter of pragmatic programming, it is a matter of survival. Research has shown that one of the greatest predictors of a teenager's ongoing growth in Christ is membership in and commitment to some sort of Christian fellowship. Simply put, *Spiritual growth means a growing sense that one is a vital part of a Christian community.*

BUILDING WITH A BLUEPRINT

One of my many areas of giftlessness is the area of home carpentry. I do not understand why God has never seen fit to equip me with this gift when he has apparently seen fit to equip me with a home in which this gift is a necessity. I recall one occasion of unabashed boldness when I announced to the family that I was going to build a back porch deck. Their response was almost instantaneous. My wife asked, "But will it be safe for the kids?" One of my daughters wisely stifled laughter, and the youngest just started crying.

By the time the deck was finished, their skepticism was entirely justified. I had done several things right: the concrete set nicely around the main posts, and the structure seemed to be strong enough to support a family cook-out. But I ran into problems in the final phases of construction. Apparently I had mismanaged my initial measurements of the four main corners of the deck, and by the time I was ready to complete the flooring and the side rails of the deck, it was obvious that the deck was out of line. I had to bend boards, patch corners, and create side pieces. I had envisioned a square deck, but I had actually constructed one that was more of a trapezoid! And it all began by my having an imbalance in one of the original four angles.

A wise builder begins with the end in mind. If our goal is to nurture students in their spiritual maturity, we need to begin with this in mind. We carefully lay out a pattern that balances the four biblical areas of Christian growth. We plan for growth to be: (1) centered on a relationship with Jesus; (2) motivated by a sense of call; (3) guided by a mature and discerning wisdom; and (4) encouraged and bolstered by a sense of community.

If we begin a program of nurturing Christian growth without making sure we have each of these four foundational areas in equal proportion, we are going to build a lop-sided youth ministry that ends up disappointingly different from what we had envisioned.

CHAPTER TWO

TEENAGERS AND GOD: THE WAY WE WERE

Defining adolescent spirituality is only the beginning. I spoke with one youth minister in the process of my writing this book who joked candidly, "Oh, I've *defined* teenage spirituality, I just can't *find* teenage spirituality." Most of us know the feeling.

Perhaps one of the reasons that the ministry of nurture can be so discouraging is that we're not completely sure what we're looking for. Anyone who has ever known the wonderful experience of parenthood will relate to the fact that it isn't always so easy to envision the finished product when it's still early in the process.

Any father who has ever been present at the miraculous moment of a birth will probably admit that when he first set eyes on that little lump of humanity emerging from the womb, variously colored purple and red and covered with afterbirth, there was at least that fleeting moment in which he thought, "Hey, it's cute! But what is it? We waited nine months for this? Put it back!"

One father confided in me that his biggest trial in parenthood was standing with his two-year-old and acting excited about the progress being made there on the toilet seat. Sometimes the process doesn't look very much like progress, but that can be deceptive. It is just such moments that lead to growth and maturity.

Quite often spiritual birth brings with it the very same kinds of bittersweet signs of progress. It's probably significant that when Paul writes to the immature Christians in the church at Galatia, his exasperation takes on the tone of an expectant parent: "My dear children, for whom I am again in the pains of childbirth until Christ is formed in you! . . . I am perplexed about you" (Galatians 4:19). It would be wonderful if youth ministry were only about those great breakthrough moments of new birth and recommitment. But there are all those months and years of care and nurture in between that begin with gestation (pre-evangelism) and continue all the way through the bumps and falls of learning to walk alone.

THE WAY WE WERE

Before you begin reading this chapter, take a moment to answer these questions:

1. *What were three significant spiritual events in your own life?* Maybe these events occurred prior to any kind of conversion experience; maybe they were post-conversion. But try to recall at least three significant events or moments when you felt an awareness of God.

In my own life, I can recall very clearly three events that were milestones in my spiritual pilgrimage. The first was a Young Life retreat I attended as a senior in high school. It was the first time I really sensed the possibility of a real and vital God. A friend, Donnie Selzer (now a pastor in California), shared with me about his personal relationship with Christ. The second was a Thanksgiving retreat with Young Life during my freshman year of college. What God began in the preceding spring and nurtured over the summer, was born that weekend; I made a conscious commitment to invite Jesus into my heart and life. The third was an Easter weekend the following April. I was down at the beach with my friends, almost hoping that I could suppress my growing faith in Christ. I heard a Christian singing group called New Directions that weekend, and through their music and personal witness, God reminded me that I was now his, and that he would not so easily let me go.

2. *Name two people who had a significant spiritual impact in your life.* They may have been Sunday school teachers, your parents, coaches, youth workers, or even peers, people who in one way or another had the effect of moving you forward in your commitment to Christ.

Unquestionably I would identify my parents as one source of powerful spiritual impact in my life. I saw their love for each other and for their children. I saw their integrity and their high moral standards. And I saw it all blended together in two people who knew how to have a good time.

Beyond parental influence, there was the notable impact of Dick Gehron, my Young Life leader in high school, whose life and witness wooed me into the kingdom of God. And then there was the life-shaping influence of J.L. and Patt Williams, whose ministry, marriage, and commitment to Christ galvanized my faith and helped me understand my identity as a child of God. It was J.L. who really had a deep ministry of nurture in my own life. (He was the culprit who nailed me for those "minor" offenses mentioned in the introduction of this book.)

3. *Try to recall one significant decision you made that was affected by your faith in Christ. Can you remember the first time that your commitment to Christ influenced a decision?*

In all honesty, this is the toughest question for me to answer. I think it may have been my decision during Easter break of my freshman year in college to stop being such a wimp about my faith in Christ. It was at that point I decided to come out of the (prayer) closet, and get up early on Easter morning, when all my other friends were asleep or hung over, so that I could celebrate the Resurrection with other believers.

You are being given the opportunity to reflect on how Christian maturity has come about in your own life. If we want to appreciate the process and wonder of spiritual nurture, this may be the best way to start. Quite often, as people take part in this kind of exercise, they make some of the following observations.

GOD DOESN'T ALWAYS ACT WHEN HE'S SUPPOSED TO

While there may have been some key memorable event in your spiritual odyssey, it is very seldom the kind of event on which we spend so much time and concern in youth ministry. It is rare that people can recall a skit that was so powerful that it changed their lives. To my knowledge, there has never been a person whose life has been changed by a Stupid Night, a Banana Bash, or any other kind of creative resource.

In fact, I can't recall a single teenager from my years in youth ministry who would say that the key spiritual event in their life was one of Duffy's Bible studies or that incredible talk Duffy gave at the Fall retreat. While most of the students I've worked with may attest to a particular speaker or sermon as being significant in their Christian journey, few could actually recount what was the topic of the sermon or the text of the study. And yet, we seem to be pre-occupied with such matters in our ministry with students.

THE BULGING TUMMY PRINCIPLE

Who knows how many times we have left the Fellowship Hall wondering why God didn't show up for youth meeting, only to discover in later months and years that the cumulative effect of those events left a deep spiritual impact on our students? It's a bit like watching the stomach of a pregnant wife for nine months and, except for sheer bulge, there aren't many signs of progress. It's easy to think from one month or one day to the next, "Well, nothing going on in there today." And then, all of a sudden . . . BIRTH.

I remember a disastrous summer camp in the White Mountains of New Hampshire when it seemed that everything that could go wrong *did* go wrong. The weather wasn't co-operative. We had some equipment problems. And there were a few moments when it seemed we were near mutiny. I remember coming home from that retreat depressed and ready to go into telemarketing.

Partially out of frustration and partially out of a sense of confusion about what went wrong, I followed up that retreat by a personal visit with each of the students who had taken part. These were not pleasant conversations. In many cases, I felt I had to confront these students with my disappointment. Not surprisingly, their response was not overwhelmingly warm and grateful. And yet somehow those confrontations and ensuing conversations became a turning point in our ministry.

Often, those of us in youth ministry make immediate judgments about which retreats, talks, Bible studies, and programs were significant for our students. But in fact, it is really the passing of time that gives us the necessary lens to discern spiritual significance.

NEGATIVES WITH A POSITIVE EFFECT

Sometimes we are surprised by how many of the key events in our spiritual growth seemed to be negative and painful at the time. I have had countless conversations with adult youth workers who recount three significant events in their own sojourn with Christ and admit that at least one of those three events seemed counter-productive at the time.

At a recent youth leader's workshop in North Carolina, one youth-worker shared how his own encounter with God came through a serious sports injury that forced him to re-evaluate his identity, his plans, and his goals. At the time, he recounted, "It seemed like a lousy break. Now I can see it was the beginning of God's restoring me to wholeness."

That is very important for us to remember in youth ministry. We are so busy protecting students from bad decisions and difficult times. It may be good that we are reminded that frequently we hear God best when we might be expecting to hear him least. John Wenham puts it this way: "God whispers in our pleasure, but shouts in our pain" (*The Goodness of God*, InterVarsity Press, 1974).

Remember that young prodigal in Luke 15:11–32? It wasn't until he was standing knee-deep in pig manure that he came to his senses and decided to return home (v. 17). No one would have thought it at the time, but that may have been the key event that brought the boy back to his father.

So many times I will ask one of my youth ministry students here at Eastern College to share with me how they came to discover Christ is real, and chose to serve him in some kind of vocational service. It's uncanny how many times I hear a student point back to what at the time could only have been described as a tragedy.

The students recount situations that must have seemed to their youth minister the final nail in their spiritual coffin. I can't help but wonder if those youth ministers have since heard that the tragedy of those high-school years was only the student's earliest labor pains before the start of a whole new life.

When God confronted Joshua at the foot of those massive Jericho walls, it must have appeared to everyone an impossible, impassable situation. To be sure, the Promised Land was so close they could almost smell it. But staring up at those awesome walls, Joshua sensed anything but victory. Confronted in Joshua 5:13 by a man standing before him "with a drawn sword in his hand," Joshua was clearly at his battle station. "Are you for us, or for our enemies?" he asked as only a military man might do.

But when this unnamed heavenly visitor identified himself as the commander of the army of the Lord, Joshua let his guard down. " 'What message does my Lord have for his servant?' The commander of the Lord's army replied, 'Take off your sandals, for the place where you are standing is holy' " (Joshua 5:15).

This is an intriguing command, to say the least. What was the point? I'm convinced God was exhibiting a vital principle here for those of us in youth ministry. For Joshua and all the world, the situation looked hopeless: we have progressed this far but we can go no further. The walls are just too high; the challenge just too steep. And it's at that point God says, "Take off your sandals, for the place where you are standing is holy."

In short, so many times the problems of growth and nurture have nothing to do with the altitude of the walls and everything to do with the attitude of the warrior. God is big enough to knock down any wall. Being involved in the spiritual nurture of teenagers requires that we keep the kind of vision that says this may look like a battleground to everybody else, but it's holy ground to God.

In the midst of those classic youth-ministry horror stories in which everything seems to go wrong, and we see no potential for growth and no forward progress, we must remember to take off our shoes. God is often at work in just these kinds of circumstances. Some day a person will remember this as a dark period in their adolescence when all looked bleak. But they will look back at that same period as a significant time in which they discovered the power of God. Understanding this principle will give us a perspective that keeps us from giving up on those in our group who seem to be struggling the most.

A PERSON-TO-PERSON CALL

The one question that most people find easiest to respond to is the question involving relationships—people who have significantly impacted their spiritual lives. In seminars all over the country, when youth workers were asked what factors were the most important in bringing them closer to Christ, and in building in them a desire to be involved with students, it was almost unanimous. Nine times out of ten, youth workers mentioned not a program, and not a resource, but a person.

For me, that person was clearly J.L. Williams, who, to this day, still occasionally calls or writes me to make sure that I am hanging tough in my walk with the Lord. To my knowledge, he never so much as cracked an IDEA book. His teaching methods were very simple and straightforward. No special learning activities or creative strategies. He just preached and taught and loved me in tangible ways.

Earl Wilson, in his excellent book, *You Try Being A Teenager* (Multnomah Press, 1982), writes that the basic premise of Christian nurture is that Christianity is best communicated by relationships. Jesus was clear in his instructions to the disciples, "By this all men will know that you are my disciples, if you love one another" (John 13:35). In the current youth-ministry environment with the proliferation of new books, programs, resources, and ideas, it is easy to overlook the importance of this principle, that the Christian faith is best communicated person-to-person.

I have been working with one youth-ministry student who, on the surface, seems to have none of the skills that would equip him for effective youth ministry: he's not that good as a speaker; he's not particularly athletic, not especially charismatic, maybe even bordering on uncool. But after a summer of interning as a youth minister in a difficult street ministry in a coastal resort city, his supervisor was remarkably positive about the work our student had done. When we probed for more information, the supervisor explained, "The kids loved him and responded to him simply because they sensed that he loved them."

You may not be a gifted programmer, a talented speaker, or a creative Bible teacher; that will not disqualify you from the ministry of nurture. On the other hand, if (with apologies to the Apostle Paul) you speak with the tongues of Tony Campolo and of Amy Grant, but have not love, you are a noisy gong and a clanging cymbal.

TEAMING UP TO MEET THE
NEEDS OF THE TEEMING MASSES

Probably no element is more critical, in terms of developing a youth ministry that nurtures spiritual growth, than adequate leadership for adequate relationships. The normal ebb and flow of youth ministry often reflects the truth of this principle.

BELL CURVE OF
MEETING RELATIONAL NEEDS

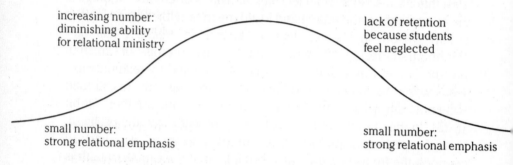

increasing number:
diminishing ability
for relational ministry

lack of retention
because students
feel neglected

small number:
strong relational emphasis

small number:
strong relational emphasis

When we are beginning a work, we start with a small number of students. Relationships are close, intimacy is real, and needs are met. For that reason, the group grows. But one must be cautious, because as the group grows, the student-to-leader ratio becomes higher and higher. The time for building relationships is crowded out by the real and perceived needs for additional programming and planning.

Unless additional adult leaders join the team so that the student-to-leader ratio is reduced, students will cease to sense the intimacy and relational attention that drew them in the first place. At that point, the attendance will slowly begin to drop off until there are once again few enough youth to permit a genuine relational ministry. Once that ministry is restored, the group grows again and the cycle continues.

A wise leader will begin to focus less attention on direct relationships with students, and more on relationships with potential leaders who can in turn have a relational ministry with the youth. "I realized in my own ministry that I was going to have to decide to be either in management or in sales," I recently heard a youth minister say. "As my ministry grew I realized I could only extend my ministry by refocusing my efforts on my leaders, so that they in turn could focus their attention on the kids. It was not an easy transition for me. I had always been right there on the front lines. But it has kept me in youth ministry over the years when I probably would have burned out otherwise."

Building a team ministry is essential to the success of any expanding ministry of nurture. If we heed it, our own experience teaches us that relationships are the key to Christian nurture. And to develop those kinds of nurturing relationships, we need to establish a team of leaders who have the time and the inclination to focus their attentions on individual students.

HOUR OF DECISION
AND DECISIONS OF OURS

We can draw at least one other observation from a survey of our own Christian journey, and that is in the area of making decisions. Quite often, people find it difficult to recall significant instances in which decisions were affected by Christ.

That difficulty ought to remind us that spiritual growth in the teenage years does not necessarily mean that there will be cataclysmic moments in which one is called to obey God rather than men (Acts 4:19, 20). My experience with teenagers is that their commitment to follow Christ is more often manifested in small and seemingly insignificant decisions.

We preach to students, hoping for that all-important hour of decision, and yet when we look back at our own walks with Christ, we observe that it was those daily, seemingly unimportant decisions that marked our progress in the faith. Perhaps we spend too much time preparing and urging our youth for the big, giant step choices, when we should spend more time rejoicing in the baby steps that are taken. It's interesting to note that Peter was quite willing to die for Jesus on that Last Supper evening (John 13:37), but when push came to shove and Peter was asked just hours after the arrest if he knew Jesus, it was clear in Peter's denial that he was not willing to live for Christ.

We can make here a second observation: just as progress in Christian growth seldom comes through one big, good decision, neither does one bad decision mean that a disciple is hopeless. Again, Peter's own example is a good one.

It's true that on the evening of Jesus' arrest, Peter's flimsy commitment to Christ was betrayed by three instances of denial. But any further study of Peter's life story as it continues into the Book of Acts reminds us that the denial chapter was not the final chapter. That one bad decision was not, in fact, the end of Peter's relationship with Jesus. As it turned out, Jesus didn't give up on Peter, and Peter didn't given up on God. Even a Peter can turn away from an earlier betrayal and become a rock for the church.

J.L. Williams, the man who poured so many hours into my own spiritual nurture, is a perfect example of a youth worker who doesn't give up when kids mess up. Danny, one young man with whom he was working, got drunk one night after a football game and ended up on J.L.'s front porch. When Dan finally got inside J.L.'s house, he proceeded to show his gratitude by throwing up on the living room carpet.

To this day, Dan recounts how J.L. held him and said, "I love you, Danny. You need to trust God to help you get free from all this. And I'm going to help you." When most of us would have given up on this apparently lukewarm Christian who evidently had no heart for God, J.L. continued to love and believe in him. Today, that young man is married to a wonderful Christian woman with whom he is building a strong family. Oh yes . . . and that young man is now a Senior Pastor with a thriving ministry in the Western North Carolina Conference of the United Methodist Church.

Anyone involved in the Christian nurture of adolescents is going to hear Jesus denied a lot more than three times. And sad to say, sometimes those speaking will be the same youth who have made to-the-death commitments. In those times of hurt and frustration, it's easy to feel that we've been betrayed too. I am haunted by how many Peters I have sent home from camp, how many I've crossed off the roster. Yet that's when we need to remember that the denial of one night—even three denials—does not constitute the final decision of a lifetime.

CHAPTER THREE

TEENAGERS AND GOD: THE WAY THEY ARE

From what we observe in our own spiritual growth, and from what we can learn through sheer experience in ministry, we know that the process of spiritual growth takes time. Jesus' parable of the soils (Mark 4:1–20) pointedly reminds us that we should be suspicious of the overnight blossom.

> Others, like seed sown on rocky places, hear the word and at once receive it with joy. But since they have no root, they last only a short time. When trouble or persecution comes because of the word, they quickly fall away. Others, like seed sown on good soil, hear the word, accept it, and produce a crop—thirty, sixty, or even a hundred times what was sown (Mark 4:16, 20).

Virtually every biblical metaphor of Christian growth alludes to a long-term process. Paul's instruction to the fledgling Christians of Colosse was no different: "So then, just as you received Christ Jesus as Lord, continue to live in him, *rooted and built up in him, and strengthened in the faith as you were taught, and overflowing with thankfulness*" (Colossians 2:6, 7).

The process of Christian nurture is the one of preparing the soil for the good seed to grow, then planting that seed, helping it to take root, and nurturing its growth so that it can reproduce itself. To be youth ministers who successfully nurture the youth in our care, we need to have some sense of what this soil preparation, planting, and rooting process looks like in the life of a teenager.

David C. Cook Publishing Company (Elgin, IL) has come out with teacher training material that provides a helpful model for thinking through this process. This model reminds us that whether we are learning about math, science, or the Christian life, we move through various layers of learning. These layers are depicted in the following diagram.

DAVID C. COOK'S
LAYERS OF LEARNING

Unawareness: Couldn't Care Less
    Awareness: Notice, But Uncertain It's True
        Interest: Think It Could Be Important
            Acceptance: Tested Against Experience—Seems To Be True
            Conviction: Important to Me and to Others
                Commitment: Overriding Importance to Me—
                      Determines How I Feel and Act

STAGE ONE:
UNAWARENESS

David C.Cook's model of learning reminds us that Christian nurture begins well before an adolescent has any kind of spiritual awareness. We often think of nurture as a process that begins only after the seed takes root, but unfortunately, that fallacy leads us to ignore the importance of the ministry of evangelism.

Nowhere in Scripture are we called to go out into all the world and make Christians; We are called to make disciples. *God* makes Christians, and people make disciples. But to have discipleship without evangelism would be like trying to nurture a plant that has never been planted.

Sometimes our neglect of this truth leads us to build a youth ministry that is ingrown, that has no vision for outreach. Jesus called his followers to be fishers of men. I don't know much about fishing, but I do know that fish rarely lunge up out of the water and jump into a net sitting on the dock. A youth-ministry program should include some hooks to bait youth with no spiritual background.

Obviously, any youth ministry would benefit from a core group of students who are really serious about Jesus, and that is a goal toward which we work. But seldom is that where we start. When a ministry is new, most of the students are not going to be serious-minded disciples; they are going to be adolescents who are virtually unaware of spiritual reality.

Part of the genius of Art Erickson's twenty-plus years of youth ministry at Park Avenue United Methodist Church in Minneapolis is that Art's program offers inner-city kids everything from computer tutor workshops, to backpacking trips in Colorado, to their annual Soul Liberation Festival on the blacktop near the church. Art has realized that if he is going to reach that teenager who is virtually unaware of God, he is going to have to first bring that teenager within the realm of his influence. And while a computer class may seem an unlikely tool for nurture, it is one way Park Avenue's youth ministry reaches out to new kids in the neighborhood. Therefore, it is the first necessary step in moving some kid closer to Jesus.

What we must understand is that if we are moving our youth forward, through the primary stages of unawareness and then into awareness, we *are* nurturing students. We *are* helping them to grow spiritually. The harvest begins with the sowing of the seed.

Sometimes we forget this principle. We hear and read about the ministries around us with huge numbers of students who are deeply spiritual, fired up about Jesus, and who list Old Testament passages under their senior picture in the yearbook, and we get discouraged. "Look at our kids. They're spiritual wimps! We must not be doing a good job." Not necessarily.

STAGE TWO:
AWARENESS

The second stage of the adolescent's spiritual odyssey is characterized by increasing awareness. At this point, the youth begins to take notice of spiritual matters, but is unconvinced of their importance. This stage of spiritual development might be likened to that point at which Jesus had spit on the eyes of the blind man of Bethsaida (a unique evangelistic strategy, not necessarily recommended by the author) so that he could see people, but they looked "like trees walking around" (Mark 8:23, 24). It's not yet sight, but it's no longer total blindness.

The key to ministry at this stage, as Jesus' own example so well illustrates, is the ministry of personal touch—meeting student's felt needs. We ought to take note of that. When I first became a Christian I had the mistaken notion that if I could just provide convincing arguments in favor of the faith, I would be able to direct people's attention to Christ. I was especially impressed at that time by the apologetics and writings of Josh McDowell in *Evidence That Demands a Verdict*, and used this resource to win a lot of arguments. Unfortunately, I didn't win many people.

In the world of today's adolescent, the evidence doesn't necessarily demand a verdict. I recall vivid conversations with Tim, a high-school student, in which I felt I had compellingly presented the logic of the resurrection of Christ. He responded with an equally compelling argument: "I don't care."

The progression to awareness may take different forms,but at its heart is personal relationship—the personal touch. Bill was fairly typical. His interest in spiritual things began, by his own account, as he watched other kids in the youth group. He noticed their love for each other, and how they were different from other kids at school. He observed this in the group leaders as well. At the time, I would never have guessed that he was doing any serious thinking at all, but he was thinking and evaluating, taking it all in.

My first indication that there was any interest at all was on a weekend retreat after a Saturday night call for decision. Bill was crying, and talked late into the night with one of our adult leaders. I began to notice that Bill was considering himself a part of our group, no longer a visitor now, but a regular. At this point he was probably following a few individual leaders and kids more than he was following Jesus, but it was progress. Finally, about a year after we had first seen Bill walk into a youth meeting, he made his own personal decision to follow Christ.

One might reasonably ask, if gaining awareness is such a relational ministry, what is the point of large, evangelistic, rally-type meetings? Good question. The answer is that large gatherings give leaders a context in which to make contact with non-Christian kids. (For more information on this kind of larger group activity, see *Creative Socials and Special Events*, Youth Specialties/Zondervan, 1986.) The bowling parties, the skate nights, and the beach trips are important because they provide for us a context in which to meet and build relationships with students who simply have no intention of showing up at a worship service or Bible study.

STAGE THREE:
INTEREST

At this point in spiritual development, the teenager is beginning to feel that this God talk may be important, but there is really no decision made yet. The apostle Paul often met with this kind of response as he preached to audiences who were largely unaware of the Christian Gospel.

His audience at the Areopagus in Athens was composed of people who were well-versed in various man-made religions and philosophies, but essentially unaware of the good news of Christ. When Paul spoke to them, their response was not surprisingly mixed. Some mocked him, some got angry, but some were interested. They wanted to hear more (Acts 17:32).

A few summers ago I spoke to a large group of teenagers at a conference in the Midwest. The kids were beginning to respond to my messages, but I was well aware that I hadn't said too much yet that genuinely stated the offense of the Gospel and the Cross or the importance of confession and repentance. The temptation was to leave it there—to more or less back off so as not to turn any of the kids off. But that would have been a mistake. With some misgivings and concern, I plunged ahead and gave a clear presentation of the Gospel. The response of the students was overwhelming; many said it was the first time they had really understood why Jesus had to die on a cross. I was glad I hadn't followed my gut instinct to wimp out.

At the point that the students begin to show some interest, we must boldly, clearly, and attractively explain the plan of the Gospel. The only real danger for those of us in youth ministry is that we allow ourselves to be intimidated and back off. Some youth workers think that the way to get kids interested in Jesus is by never mentioning his name. There is such fear in some quarters of turning off our youth, that we never turn them on.

No one is suggesting that we be rude or pushy. We need to be upfront, honest, and straightforward, answering the questions and hearing the doubts. Even if we do all of that, there will still be some teenagers who just aren't ready yet. They may mock us, or they may just disappear. But there will be others who are interested in hearing more.

STAGE FOUR:
ACCEPTANCE

By this stage, youth are beginning to test some of what they are hearing against experience. They begin to say, "This may be true." This is acceptance. It is not wholehearted affirmation, but it is progress.

The ministry of nurture, at this point, will consist of prayer and encouragement. One of the major sources of encouragement for students struggling with whether to accept Christ or not is hearing from their peers about how Christ can make a difference in life.

Some of us in youth ministry have gotten so sophisticated in recent years that we overlook the impact of a good old-fashioned personal testimony. And that's too bad. From what we are learning about the ways that teenagers make decisions, it is clear that they find personal stories and testimonies far more persuasive than carefully constructed theological proofs (for more information see Bolt and Myers's *The Human Connection*, InterVarsity Press, 1984).

It is also critical at this point that the teenager becomes integrally involved in some form of Christian community or fellowship. Christian nurture must take into account the supreme importance of peer influence on one's spiritual growth. The chart on the following page suggests how peer influence can be used positively at this stage of spiritual development to help a student move forward.

The chart helps us to see that just as teenagers conform in negative ways to gain group respect, the first stages of acceptance of spiritual truth may also be based primarily on a desire to be accepted by a

USING POSITIVE PEER INFLUENCE
FOR SPIRITUAL GROWTH

Level of Development	Evidence	Suggested Action
1. Conformity to maintain group respect	"Everybody's doing it"	Build positive peer support group.
2. Development of subjective standards	"I just feel it is right"	Strengthen positive peer support (individuals or group) and establish resource of support data.
3. Choices based on objective data	"I'm doing this because . . . "	Provide individual group support for integration of the objective with the subjective.
4. Internalization of moral conviction		

(This chart is taken from David C. Cook youth-ministry training materials and is used by permission)

peer group. This being the case, an important dimension of nurture at this point is building a youth-group environment in which it is okay, normal, and even desirable to be identified as a Christian.

I recently spoke at a large youth conference in Southern California, and I was impressed with the way the songleaders created in that group a positive peer pressure. Using clever hand motions, strong up-front motivation, a wise choice of songs, and sheer mob influence, the leaders made that room a place where it was—at least for that period of time—cool to sing and worship the name of the Lord.

That is one of the benefits of large youth conventions or Jesus festivals. They create an environment in which the peer pressure is positive. While it's possible for a teenager to hide in the mob and think that following the crowd is the same as following Christ, it is a step up from a teenager following the wrong crowd.

Surrounded by peers who are working through the same spiritual truths, the next stage in the teenager's acceptance comes in the form of subjective standards. The individual student begins to acquire some warm fuzzies, some feelings about God that are warm and positive. They are not convictions, and they are easily swayed, but they are signs of progress.

The best way to nurture this subjective commitment is by continued exposure to positive peer support through retreats, small group ministry, and sharing groups. But beyond that, we need to attempt to add biblical teaching and content to the equation. In short, we need to help these kids find reasons for what they are feeling, to understand why they are feeling some of what they are feeling. (Serendipity House, Littleton, Colorado provides some excellent resources for this kind of interaction.)

Eventually, we will want to move the youth into the third stage of acceptance, in which they begin to formulate beliefs based more on the objective truth of the faith than on their feelings (See chapter six, "A Faith That Affects the Heart and the Head.")

Unfortunately, this is a transfer that seldom takes place. The kids in the youth group believe in God because other kids around them believe in God. The problem, of course, is that these students will eventually find themselves around other groups of people—and their patterns and lifestyle may not be as Christ-centered. A faith based on warm fuzzies will eventually cool down.

That is why building groups and sharing feelings are no substitute for sound biblical teaching and the communication of Christian truth. We are trying to build people whose faith is based on convictions, even if they must stand alone in those convictions.

STAGE FIVE: CONVICTION

This is the point at which the moral or spiritual conviction is internalized: "This is what I believe even if everyone around me thinks I'm a jerk." A conviction is a belief held firmly enough that we are convinced of its importance not only to ourselves, but to others (For an expanded discussion of just what this conviction looks like, see Section Two of this book.)

Keith was a student in the youth group who showed conviction. Everybody expected the usual go-for-your-dreams speech when he stood up that hot June evening to deliver the valedictorian speech at his commencement. What they got instead was Keith's story, in plain words, about how he had come to know Jesus, and about how Jesus was helping him reshape his dreams and his plan to fit God's plan. Keith stood up in front of his entire class, and hundreds of parents and said, "Here I stand for Jesus." That is genuine conviction.

STAGE SIX:
COMMITMENT

By this final stage, spiritual development has progressed to the point that it determines our feelings and our actions. Obviously, just as there is a progression leading up to this stage of commitment, there is a progression of growth *within* this stage of commitment. As someone said, "We receive all of Christ at the moment of conversion; then we spend the rest of our lives allowing Christ to receive all of us."

This isn't necessarily because of hypocrisy or indecision. Especially with teenagers, this will be in part the result of immaturity. Just because adolescents make firm and real commitments to Christ doesn't mean that they will suddenly begin acting like adults, listening to Gaither music and wearing leisure suits. Christian teenagers are still teenagers.

When I first said to my wife that I loved her—on our second date—I really meant it. I was sincere. But when I vow my love to her now after sixteen years of marriage, it means decidedly more. That's not because I was insincere on that second date. Come on, now. It's just that when I pledged my all to her sixteen years ago, I wasn't really aware of all of me that there was to pledge. Sixteen years of living together, facing life together, and raising children together have helped expose new areas of me that I need to surrender to our love.

So it is with that fourteen or seventeen-year-old kid who gives his or her all to Christ. That's a real commitment. But the years will show new areas to surrender and new commitments to make.

LITTLE BY LITTLE

Our youth group used to sing a song that had the following chorus:

Little by little everyday,

Little by little in every way,
Jesus is changing me . . .

That little song holds an important spiritual truth for people who desire to nurture the spiritual growth of teenagers. When we talk about a student making a commitment to Christ, it sounds quick and easy—just like when we talk about a farmer "growing his crops." But that quick and easy phrase betrays the fact that growth takes time, sweat, patience, and prayer.

The encounter between a teenager and his God is a long road that may begin with relative unawareness and progress through long, seemingly endless stages before it blossoms into genuine conviction and commitment. Peter hints at this process in 2 Peter 1:3–8.

His divine power has given us everything we need for life and godliness through our knowledge of him who called us by his own glory and goodness. Through which he has given us his very great and precious promises, so that through them you may participate in the divine nature and escape the corruption in the world caused by evil desires. For this very reason, make every effort to add to your faith goodness; and to goodness, knowledge; and to knowledge, self-control; and to self-control, perseverance; and to perseverance, godliness; and to godliness, brotherly kindness; and to brotherly kindness, love. For if you possess these qualities in increasing measure, they will keep you from being ineffective or unproductive in your knowledge of our Lord Jesus Christ.

That's the biblical pattern of spiritual growth. It's not quick or easy. It takes God years to raise an oak tree, but he can make a mushroom overnight. Most of us in youth ministry have put in years waiting on the nuts in our groups to do something. In time, perhaps they will. For now, those of us involved and committed to a ministry of nurture with teenagers need to be reminded that progress is a process.

SECTION
TWO

REAL-LIFE STUDENT DISCIPLESHIP

CHAPTER FOUR
FIRST-HAND FAITH

At the pro shop in the club where I play racquetball there is a framed cartoon of the Avid Racquetball Player. He has eyes that look two different directions simultaneously, a huge nose swollen from running into the side walls of the court, tennis shoes with snow tire tread for quick stops, and legs that are black and blue on the back side from being hit with the opponent's kill shots. It is the ultimate statement of how the committed racquetball player is supposed to look.

How would an artist depict the Teenage Youth Groupie? Maybe a kid with an egg in her armpit and a *Student Bible* in her hand, wearing an Amy Grant T-shirt and a smile-God-loves-you button and shorts that advertise some youth mission project or beach trip. Our groupie would have an extra large throat that is swollen from having so much information and doctrine shoved down it, knees that are banged up and scratched from ridiculous games, and a rear end molded to the shape of the seat on a church bus. Strapped to her body would be a shovel for work projects, a guitar for sing-alongs, a tape player for Christian music, a backpack, skis, surfboard, volleyball, and a Bill Gothard notebook. Such a picture would be the ultimate statement of youth groupiness.

But how would we profile a teenage disciple? What would they look like? Before we begin to draw in this profile, take the following short personal survey about discipleship in general.

CHARACTERISTICS OF A TRUE DISCIPLE

Working from the list on the following page, rank the top ten most important characteristics that you would expect to see in a real-life disciple. (One is most important. Ten is least important.)

_____ 1. Careful student of the Scriptures

_____ 2. Zealous and active in their stand for God

_____ 3. Appetite for worship and prayer

_____ 4. Consistent in worship attendance

_____ 5. Practices Scripture memorization

_____ 6. Not afraid of public prayer

_____ 7. Active in affairs of local church

_____ 8. Fasts regularly

_____ 9. Has a desire to stand against blasphemy and ungodliness

_____ 10. Has a firm grasp of basic, foundational theological truths

When other youth ministers across the country have taken this survey, they've given high priority to everything from recognizing the importance of Scripture, to having a public and bold faith, to being active in the worship and ministry of a local church. And to be sure, these are all important characteristics of real-life discipleship.

But the characteristics cited above have one factor in common. They are all traits and behaviors characteristic, not of Jesus' disciples, but rather, of Jesus' most vocal opponents, the Pharisees. In fact, the irony is that the traits we most often identify with real-life discipleship are the very traits that we seldom see in the lives of Jesus' real-life disciples.

Even more puzzling is the observation that in the lives of Jesus' disciples as they are documented in the Gospels, there is a lot of behavior that is not disciple-like. For example, one rarely hears a youth minister aspire to build a youth group of kids who would fall asleep during the prayer time. But when given a glimpse of Jesus' disciples during those final hours before his arrest, we see Jesus praying so earnestly in prayer that he sweats blood. Meanwhile, the three disciples who were probably closest to him are sound asleep in a flower bed, perhaps, at best, dreaming about prayer! These are real-life disciples? **People will know you are my disciples by the ears you cut off each other?**

What this teaches us is that discipleship in the real world doesn't always fit the nice, neat, pat formulas that we commonly work with in ministry. If our goal is to nurture and disciple a group of teenagers, we need to begin by rethinking what a real-life disciple looks like.

While almost any person reading this book would grant the importance of the traits and characteristics we've listed above, it's critical that we look to Scripture for some basic guidelines to help us shape a more accurate profile of discipleship. The Bible suggests two helpful principles for defining discipleship in our day:

1. *Real-life discipleship is what happens between meetings.*

Probably, the greatest indicators of which kids in the youth group are genuine disciples are those behaviors that most of us, as youth ministers, will never see: the actions that take place after they've left the Youth Room, driven out of the church parking lot, and returned to their regular environment.

What are they like in school, at home, in the lunchroom, on dates, at parties, in the locker room, or in their after-school job? Were we to see them in those settings, we would have a much more accurate reading of their spiritual commitment. In short, watching the kids interact on the youth retreat, or observing them as they participate in a youth choir rehearsal or a Bible study, only tells part of the story. Real-life discipleship is what happens between all those neat youth-group meetings.

Cheryl was a junior at the high school. In a lot of ways, she was just like every other student at Jessup County High School. She didn't like cafeteria food. She struggled with trigonometry—a lot. She ran cross-country. And, she liked guys—a lot.

Cheryl told me of a conversation with another girl at school who had been wrestling with some problems. Cheryl listened to her problems and showed concern for her. Cheryl also told this girl about how Jesus was working in her own life, and how very much he wanted to work in hers.

What I found so exciting about that brief episode is that it happened when I wasn't around. We weren't doing a series on witnessing. This wasn't a group activity. It was Cheryl deciding on her own to share her faith. It said more about her than all of the times she spoke up in youth group or in Bible study. This time, she was speaking up at school in a setting where she might have been strongly tempted to keep quiet about her faith.

Mike was one of those students who would raise his hands at prayer time and make a completely sincere prayer request for the healing of a friend—and then go out after the meeting with his girlfriend to do some laying on of hands of his own. He would be the one on retreats to come forward at the invitation and weep out a confession in the presence of the whole youth group. But when back at school in the locker room or out on the playing field, those tears and that confession would be long forgotten. It was business as usual.

One of God's strongest rebukes to King Saul and the people of Israel was in 1 Samuel 15:22, following a service of sacrifice that on the surface looked wonderfully spiritual. At first glance, it looked as if Saul was Mr. Faithful. By his own account, " 'I did obey the Lord,' Saul said. 'I went on the mission the Lord assigned me. I completely destroyed the Amalekites and brought back Agag their king' " (1 Samuel 15:20). Surely this kind of religious activity merited some kind of pin or plaque or T-shirt.

> *But the prophet Samuel was not impressed.*
> Does the Lord delight in burnt offerings and sacrifices, as much
>   as in obeying the voice of the Lord?
> To obey is better than sacrifice, and to heed is better than the fat
>   of rams.
> For rebellion is like the sin of divination, and arrogance like the
>   evil of idolatry.
> Because you have rejected the word of the Lord, he has rejected
>   you as king (1 Sam. 15:22–23).

Reading Saul's pious testimony, one can almost imagine how it might play out in a youth-group setting. A student proclaims, "I went forward at the invitation on the fall retreat; I took part in the Mission Trip project; and I participated in the big bonfire ceremony where we got rid of all of our Van Halen tapes." That kind of testimony would have most parents, deacons, and pastors in tears. But the real indication of discipleship is a continued pattern of obedience, even when no one is watching or listening.

2. *Real-life discipleship is marked more by footprints than by monuments.*

One of the mistakes that we make in youth ministry is defining as a mark of discipleship what I call monumental experiences. When students respond to an invitation at the end of a service; when they raise their hands as a sign of deeper commitment—these are monumental experiences. They tend to stand out on the horizon of a youth ministry as being episodes in which God worked in some special way among our youth.

Most of us have witnessed last-night campfires when a speaker would challenge kids who are really serious about Jesus to come forward and stand here next to the fire. Or he might say, "If you're really willing to repent and follow Christ, come forward and throw a piece of wood into the fire." (Or the big one: "If you're really serious about Jesus tonight, just come up here and stand in this fire.") When students respond in these kind of monumental experiences, we tend to identify them as the "real" disciples in our youth group.

But identifying true disciples based on such reactions approach betrays a biblical picture of discipleship that is weighted more on the side of a long-term commitment than a one-time decision. In *A Long Obedience in the Same Direction* (InterVarsity Press, 1980), Eugene Peterson makes the point that more often than not, real discipleship is marked not by the monument, but by the footprint. The biblical picture of discipleship is a picture of forward motion: a pilgrimage, a marathon, a journey—not an arrival.

The monumental approach to discipleship says, "This is where it happened" or "This is when it happened" or "I finally made it." While there is a sense in which conversion can happen in this abrupt, monumental way, discipleship never can. For discipleship, the more appropriate symbol is a footprint that says, "This is where I was when I continued to move forward."

Surely, this is what Paul was talking about in Philippians 3:12–15:

> Not that I have already obtained all this, or have already been made perfect, but I press on to take hold of that for which Christ Jesus took hold of me. Brothers, I do not consider myself yet to have taken hold of it. But one thing I do: Forgetting what is behind and straining toward what is ahead, I press on toward the goal to win the prize for which God has called me heavenward in Christ Jesus. All of us who are mature should take such a view of things.

The reason this principle is so important in shaping our profile of real discipleship is that if we neglect it, we run the risk of encouraging our students to worship an experience, to look back at that one weekend, or that one worship service as being an ending, when in fact God intends it to be only a beginning. Church youth groups are full of students who have been urged so much to get saved that they have never realized God wants to continue his saving work in us everyday—refining, strengthening, making us into his likeness (Romans 5:9–11). It's an ongoing, lifelong process.

If we understand the process of discipleship as a sequence of footprints in the right direction, we can understand how Jesus would dare to refer to a motley group of jealous, doubting, thick-headed, spiritually-impaired followers as his disciples. And I don't know about you, but that gives me some hope for the kids I work with.

The Greek word for *discipleship* means *learner*, not *expert*. These disciples weren't there yet, but they were following Jesus, and moving in the right direction.

It is a monument mindset that leaves us justified and petrified. The footprint mindset reminds us that a student's spiritual position is not nearly as important as his spiritual direction. And we won't really be able to see that in one episode in the front of the church or around the campfire. That kind of discipleship will only be manifest over the long haul.

Beginning with these two over-arching premises, we are ready to focus more specifically on the marks of real discipleship in the life of a teenager.

TEENAGE DISCIPLESHIP IS MARKED
BY A FIRSTHAND FAITH

One of the first tasks in the Christian nurture of teenagers is to help them come to the point where they possess their own faith.

Chris had been active in the youth group from almost the first day of my ministry in his church. He was present for every meeting, willing to volunteer for extra activities, and almost always eager to spend extra time with me, whether that was to throw a frisbee, to participate in a work project, or to be involved in small group discipleship. I had big plans and high hopes for Chris. He was everything a youth minister would hope to see in one of his kids.

That's why I was so disappointed after four years with Chris when he graduated from our youth group and put his spiritual life on hold. I knew that Chris had some weaknesses and blind spots, but I had always felt that if anybody in our youth group would go out there and make waves for the Kingdom of God, Chris would. And now Chris the wavemaker was just treading water.

As I thought about my ministry with Chris, it finally dawned on me that perhaps one of the reasons he had fallen so far short of my dreams for him was just that: they were MY dreams for him. He had never been forced to forge a vision and faith of his own. Chris didn't need to have faith; I had enough faith for both of us. He didn't need to make his own commitment to Christ; I was all too willing to let him borrow mine. Chris had never developed a firsthand allegiance to God.

PIAGET, FOWLER,
AND YOUTH MINISTRY

In virtually every college psychology class, students become acquainted with Jean Piaget's theories of cognitive development—theories that evaluate the ways in which our thinking changes as we move through various stages of life. For example, Piaget notes that children who are in the early years of elementary school are concrete thinkers. They accept as fact what they are told by the adults around them. They don't question; they don't ask, "Why?" or "What if?" or

"How can that be true if this is true?" Their world makes sense; it all adds up. Their thinking is concrete.

As the child begins to move into the years of early adolescence, something happens. He begins to think in a new way. Piaget describes this new stage as a stage of formal operations. In short, the child begins thinking abstractly. He starts to raise new questions and struggle with new issues. As any parent who has ended a conversation with their junior higher with "Because I said so—that's why" will tell you that these kids are becoming less willing to accept the authoritarian answers that seemed satisfactory a few years earlier.

On many occasions I've had to reassure junior high volunteers who unknowingly witness this cognitive shift and are discouraged by what they are seeing. They begin working with a sixth or seventh grade student who seems to believe in God and respect the authority of the leader. And by the time the kid is in ninth grade, he seems to have gone backward, lost his faith, and become less responsive to leadership. On the surface, it's not exactly a success story. But what these leaders actually may be seeing is a normal process of development in which this adolescent is beginning to think differently about the world around him.

Parents, youth leaders, and other adult figures often view this new skeptic as a rebel. In reality these pre-teens and young adolescents are simply beginning to think independently—to recompute some of the old equations and see if they still come up with the same answers. They are stretching new mental muscles that allow them to think in new ways about old answers. Instead of stopping with "Why?" they might begin to ask, "Why not?"

In James Fowler's seminal work, *The Stages of Faith: The Psychology of Human Development and the Quest for Meaning* (Harper & Row, 1981), Fowler writes about the fact that just as we go through stages in our cognitive or intellectual development, so do we go through stages in the development of our faith. While one may not agree with everything Fowler says, some of his insights help us to think about the ways we help teenagers nurture a personal faith.

Based on his interviews with religious people of all ages, Fowler believes that there are basically six stages of faith:

Stage One: Intuitive-Projective Faith (4–8 years old)

At this earliest stage, Fowler found that children generally get their ideas about God and religion from the adults closest to them. And so, for the most part, their ideas about God and faith will be formulated by watching and listening to their parents. No one tells them they should use this approach. It is intuitive. Often, young children will get their earliest impressions of God by projecting their impressions of their own mother or father.

We probably ought to realize that we have kids in our youth groups whose view of God has never progressed beyond this stage of faith. This is particularly important in light of the tragic data surrounding molestation and sexual abuse in American families. With one out of four girls in this country likely to be abused by the age of eighteen, we can't afford to forget that our talk about God as Father may leave some of our youth with very negative images.

I remember one student in my first full-time youth-ministry position who could not accept the fact that God could love him. He felt he was too far gone, beyond even the love of God. Donnie was a pretty typical teenager—slightly on the freak side: long hair, total jean wardrobe, etc. No matter what I said, it seemed he was unable to accept that God could love him as he was. Then one day his father shared with me a conversation they had.

The two of them were talking about all of the parts of Donnie's life that his father found distasteful: the hair, the music, the wardrobe, the lifestyle, etc. And his father was saying, "Son, I'm only saying all of this because I love you and I care about you." At which point, Donnie interrupted, "But Dad, can you love me if I never change? Can you love me just the way I am?" It was a hard conversation for Donnie's Dad to relate to me. We had to talk about how to lovingly communicate acceptance to our children even when we cannot honestly communicate approval of all they do.

I began to understand that Donnie's view of the heavenly Father had been influenced heavily by an earthly father who had unintentionally communicated to his son, "I cannot accept you as you are because I do not approve of all that you do." Donnie had never left that intuitive-projective stage of faith.

Stage Two: Mythic-Literal Stage (6–7 to 11–12 years old)

In the mythic-literal stage of faith, Fowler found that children were beginning to give attention to the rest of the world. They were beginning to distinguish between what is real and what is fantasy. Most of us remember what it was like to huddle together in the cafeteria in fourth grade and have heated discussions about Santa Claus and the Tooth Fairy.

Fowler found that kids at this age are still a bit threatened by the uncertainties of the world around them, and that while they are beginning to sort through their beliefs, their faith in God seems to give them a sense of security. Typically, in interviews, children at this stage viewed God as both faithful and lawful. The years to come will test that belief, but in the meantime, the questions that do arise can still be answered.

One of my first professional discoveries in youth ministry was how easy it was to get junior high kids to make some kind of commitment to Christ. Unfortunately, one of my second professional discoveries was that those commitments don't always last a long time. And that's not because the junior highers are insincere; it is because they are moving back and forth between concrete of thinking that readily accepts adult direction, and the abstract thinking that is characterized by more freedom.

Stage Three: Synthetic-Conventional Stage (12 years–adulthood)

As young teens move into their junior high years, they progress through what Fowler describes as the Synthetic-Conventional stage of faith. It is synthetic, not in the sense that it is phony, but in the sense that it is a faith shaped by interpersonal relationships. It is a conventional faith, shaped essentially by the attitudes of those with whom one finds oneself at any given time.

It is probably this stage of faith that youth workers find most exasperating, because they will find themselves working with students who on Sunday night seem to be a spiritual dynamos, but around their unchurched friends on Friday night they blow it big time.

Jenny was one such girl in my own ministry. She seemed right at home when she was among her peers at youth group, singing solos in youth choir, giving the right answers in Bible study, and participating willingly in all of the activities and discussions. But because her faith was at the synthetic-conventional stage, she also fit in all too well with her non-Christian peers at the Friday night party, giving the answers that seem to be expected in that setting and willingly participating in those activities as well. In short, at this stage of immature belief, students learn to compartmentalize their faith so that Sunday's commitment doesn't impact Monday's lifestyle. As Fowler points out, even some adults never develop beyond this kind of second-hand faith.

If we forget that real discipleship is a function of what takes place between the meetings, we will be easily fooled by kids at this stage in their faith development. While in our presence, they make the right sounds and go through the right motions, so they must be the real thing. But just because kids behave appropriately at youth group and never cause trouble does not mean that they will act that way Monday through Saturday night.

Probably, the greatest danger at this stage of faith development is that students will fall into the trap of having a second-hand faith. They will follow God because their particular group seems to be following God. But we cannot afford to be satisfied with a shared commitment. Because unfortunately, once they graduate from high school, they will likely be surrounded by a whole new group to follow, and that group may not be following God at all.

Stage Four: Individuative-Reflective Faith (17–18 to adulthood)

The last of Fowler's six stages that concerns us in youth ministry is this fourth stage, the individuative-reflective stage of faith. According to Fowler, it is finally at this point that the believer has a firsthand faith. It is individuative in that it is a faith of their own, and it is reflective in the sense that those who move into this stage have taken time to reflect on what they actually and personally believe. This is where we are attempting to move the students in our ministries.

As Scott Peck put it in his best-selling work, *The Road Less Traveled* (Simon & Schuster, 1980),

One of our problems is that few of us have developed any distinctive personal life. Everything about us seems second-hand, even our emotions. In many cases we have to rely on second-hand information in order to function. I accept the word of a physician, a scientist, a farmer on trust. I do not like to do this. I have to because they possess vital knowledge of living of which I am ignorant. Second-hand information concerning the state of my kidneys, the effects of cholesterol, and the raising of chickens, I can live with. But when it comes to questions of meaning, purpose, and death, second-hand information will not do. I cannot survive on a second-hand faith in a second-hand God. There has to be a personal word, a unique confrontation, if I am to live.

HOW WE CAN NURTURE A FIRSTHAND FAITH

Too many youth programs attempt to program their kids into a relationship with God, when what those youth really need is time and space to build their own relationship with God. A lot of us end up building youth groups that know more about Amy Grant's faith than their own, and more about our walk with God than their own.

That means that the best way to nurture a firsthand faith in our students is to occasionally and consciously program *no* program. In other words, provide opportunities for the students to reflect on an individual basis about their own faith. An example of a way to do this is a day-long trip to the mountains, the beach, or just some park that takes your students away from the normal interruptions of everyday life.

There is nothing particularly new about this idea. Kids are usually so busy that they really have little time to be reflective about anything, let alone their Christian faith. But the key here is going to be the way we use that time out on the beach or in that mountain meadow. If we are like most youth ministers, as soon as we arrive at the picnic spot and all the students unload the bus, we are immediately smothering them with optional activities and organized games. In short, we're not giving them adequate time for reflection and thought.

Here are some alternatives to the typical planned, crammed social activities.

1. Journaling

In my own ministry, I have found that journaling is a particularly good way to facilitate student reflection. I knew one high-school student who would have hyperventilated at the thought of writing a five-page paper for school. But every week he faithfully wrote several pages of entries in his personal journal. And in doing so, he was forced to reflect on and articulate his own personal faith.

We can facilitate the journaling process by giving students guidelines and suggestions. For example:

- encourage students to read a Psalm a day, and jot down their thoughts about what they've read;
- encourage students to write their own psalms;
- use some of the various tools available to aid students and stimulate them in their journaling. The *Grow For It Journal* published by Youth Specialties (1224 Greenfield Dr., El Cajon, CA 92021) is an excellent example of the kind of tool that incites and invites personal reflection.

2. Directed Meditation

It was during my freshman year of college that I read a small booklet by Robert Boyd Munger entitled, *My Heart Christ's Home*. Taking part in a Young Life camp, we had been sent out into the morning air to find a place in the valley and be by ourselves while we read through this little booklet. In the quiet and beauty of that morning, I was deeply moved by what I read. Later that night, I prayed to invite Jesus into my heart.

This kind of exercise in directed meditation simply requires that you give students two things: 1) Something to think about; and 2) time and space for thinking. The something to think about can be a written piece (*My Heart Christ's Home* is available from InterVarsity Press, 5200 Main St., Downers Grove, IL, 60515), or some specific verbal instructions.

The key here is that you don't simply send students out into the woods and tell them to think about just anything. Experience has taught me that, given some guidance, students actually appreciate the time to be alone and think. Kids are seldom quiet in their normal everyday lifestyle. When they are, God can really work.

With my own youth groups, I have used articles from *Campus Life* magazine, or particular passages of Scripture with a few seed thoughts. The only guidelines for using a written piece would relate to length. Due to reading abilities and attention spans, an article for directed meditation should rarely take more than twenty minutes to read completely.

Beyond that qualification, the only other factor in choosing an article would be that it should have content that is not so much educational as it is "realizational." That is, the point of reading the article is not so much to teach your students some new truth as it is to help them realize some new truth about themselves and their relationship with God.

3. Path Finding

I attended a seminary on a campus that had once been a training school for young Catholic men considering the priesthood, and I observed that within the Catholic tradition, landscape and space were used to provoke meditation. There were various stations of meditation throughout the campus that obviously had been prepared to stimulate thoughtful prayer and serious contemplation. I guess I never really believed this would work until I tried it with my own youth group. Along with my volunteers, I developed a path of meditation that would direct students to various locations around the vicinity of our church. And then, at each location, students were given thought-provoking questions that coincided with the particular station. For example:

Station One—A Bank: "What are you banking on in your life? What is your security?"

Station Two—A Cemetery: "All of the people buried here had dreams, hopes, and plans just like you do. Now that their lives are over, many of them have left behind a legacy of families and friends and lives in which they've invested themselves. For others, some of whom made important decisions and lots of money, all that they have left behind is what stands on the top of their grave. When your life is over, what do you hope to leave behind?"

Station Three—Construction Site: "What are you 'building' with your life? What will this 'building' accomplish? Will it be a monument to yourself or to God? Will it be a place of recreation? Worship? Are you 'building' something that will outlive you?"

Station Four—Service Station: "What fuels your life? What motivates you and gets you moving?"

Students were given notepads and encouraged to jot down their thoughts at each site. Eventually, we gathered back at the church, and allowed students to share some of their insights.

Another youth minister has used this same concept and takes his students annually on A Tour of Your Life. It is a day that begins in the morning in the maternity ward of a hospital, where the guided discussion talks about the kinds of dreams and fears that their parents might have had for them on the day that they were born. Then the tour takes them through various stages of life, stopping at an elementary school, the high school/junior high school, a college, two or three local work places, a retirement home and finally ends up at a funeral home.

At each stop, students are encouraged to record their thoughts in a journal, or share them in group discussion. With each location, just as with each stage of life, there are questions and issues that are offered up for meditation. The genius of ending the day at a funeral home is that most funeral homes have a small chapel that can be used for some sort of worship experience or service of commitment.

4. Personal Parable

This is an activity that will work well whether you are meeting in a church building, camping out in the woods, or simply spending a day in a park. Give students about thirty minutes or less in which they are instructed to go out and find some object that describes their relationship with God, or tells something about who they are, or illustrates some lesson they've learned about the Christian life. Tell them to go out alone, and agree that there will be thirty minutes of silence.

Obviously, it isn't so important what students bring back. I have seen students use anything from an empty canteen to a rock to a trailside flower that had been stepped on. When students gather again, allow them to share their personal parables. The key is to help students talk in their own words about their Christian life.

5. Small Groups

Small groups can be a wonderful place for kids to explore their personal faith. The vital key here, however, is that these groups need to be sharing-oriented, not Bible study-oriented. I have been a part of small groups in which we had just another Bible study with fewer participants, or a sermon given to five people. Small group leaders should be reminded that the purpose of this kind of group is not to do Bible studies with a group of people, but to do people-studies by using the Bible.

There are published resources for this kind of sharing. Lyman Coleman's *Serendipity* materials are excellent for this purpose (Littleton, Colorado). The key is finding material which focuses less on the Bible study and more on the Bible student. Otherwise, it is quite possible for a teenager to sit through a small group, and know that the Bible says *this*, and that Rahab believes *that*—but never have to reckon with and verbalize what they personally believe. We need to study the Bible, but sometimes we benefit by using the Bible to study ourselves.

The following is an example of a people-study based on the Bible:

Have students read Isaiah 40:31: "Those who hope in the Lord will renew their strength. They will soar on wings like eagles, they will run and not grow weary, they will walk and not be faint."

In your small group, respond to this question: Which of the following best describes your relationship with the Lord in light of that passage? a. *An Eagle*—soaring to new heights by his power; b. *A Mockingbird*—making the right sounds, talking the right talk, but it's not for real; c. *A Turkey*—I feel like a loser; can't seem to get off the ground; d. *A Chicken*—I'm a Christian, but nobody really knows it; I'm sort of shy about taking a stand for Jesus among my buddies; e. *A Buzzard*—I know the Bible calls sin the way of death, but it still looks pretty tasty to me.

5. Use Questions

The activities suggested above work best when we communicate to our students that the youth group is a place for questions of faith as well as statements of faith. Programs like confirmation class too often help students to reflect on what the church believes. But if we are going to nurture a firsthand faith, the real issue is what that kid believes. Make ample use of questions that force students to consider what they actually believe about the Christian faith.

Why do we pray? Why is there evil in a world created by a loving and all-powerful God? Do we really have freedom to make decisions if God is all-powerful? Why is it that bad things seem to happen to good people and good things seem to work out for bad people? Don't settle for the pat answers. Watch out for kids speaking Christianese. Push them to articulate their own thoughts in their own words.

FIRSTHAND FAITH

The one thread that runs through each of the above exercises is that they encourage kids to talk about *their* faith. Helping students develop a firsthand faith will mean that we must use strategies that will help teenagers question, probe, and reflect on their own walk with Christ. Perhaps the best way to understand the youth worker's role in this process is to think back to those thrilling days of yesteryear when you were a little child going on a trip with your parents.

Inevitably, your mom or dad would come into the room to help you pack your bag, or perhaps to pack it without your help at all. My mom would load up with all kinds of items I knew I would never use: a raincoat, my seersucker shorts, a tie, etc. But I never complained. I figured, "She's the one that will have to carry it. Let her put in whatever she wants!"

But eventually, we came to a point of showdown. It was the summer of my tenth year and I was going away to summer camp—all by myself. Mom came into the room to begin packing my things. First the raincoat, then the rainboots. On and on it went. Finally I protested: "Mom, I don't need seven pairs of underwear. We're only going to be there for two weeks! I don't want to take all this stuff."

What happened that day was a significant stage in my development as a growing kid. I began to realize that from now on, I was going to be responsible for what was in this bag. I was going to have to bear its weight. I would have to carry my own load. And that was when I decided to exercise more choice about exactly what went in there!

Very much the same thing happens with the teenagers in our youth group. They move through the early years of Sunday school and confirmation, and we as parents and Sunday school teachers, load them up with all of these neat Christian beliefs. And that's great. The kids don't complain. After all, they rarely face situations in which they will have to bear the burden of these beliefs. So there's no problem.

But all of a sudden the young adolescent discovers the rules are changing a bit. He is going to have to bear the weight of these beliefs. He is going to have to assume responsibility for these beliefs and doctrines and all the consequences that will come with them. At the same time, he is beginning to think differently about some of the pat answers he's been given.

That is when our task as youth ministers is very important. In order to help teenagers build a firsthand faith, we must stop trying to cram beliefs in their baggage, to fill their doctrinal stockings and just expect them to carry it because we said so. Rather, we must use questions and strategies that will help them to unpack that faith baggage they've been working with, re-examine what is in there and why it is in there, and then help them to repack it.

When they have packed that bag for themselves, they will be much more willing to bear its responsibilities and consequences.

FIRSTHAND FAITH—
FIRST PRIORITY

That is why our major task in the nurture of teenagers is helping them to develop a firsthand faith—encouraging them to say yes to Jesus, instead of nagging them to say no to something that is "not Jesus." Any nurture of genuine discipleship must begin here with helping students to own their own faith. But as important as this is, it is only the beginning.

CHAPTER FIVE
A FRESH NEW LOOK AT PEER PRESSURE

We know that one of the key influences in the faith formation of teenagers is peer pressure—that their faith is greatly affected by interpersonal relationships. That being the case, one of the important elements of nurturing a firsthand (or, as Fowler put it, an individuative-reflective) faith is coming to grips with peer pressure.

THE PROBLEM
WE LOVE TO HATE

Everybody seems to relish a good hit at peer pressure these days. When you're driving past a dozen teenagers hanging out in a store parking lot long after closing time, perched on the hoods of their cars and puffing on various and sundry smokable products (some legal, some illegal), it's with perverse pleasure that we scowl through the car window and utter some quick epithet about teenagers and peer pressure. On a quick drive-by, the lot full of teenagers parked, perched, and puffing makes peer pressure seem like a villain.

And probably there is some reason for us to suspect that peer pressure has a part to play in this assemblage. Certainly, a dozen teenagers do not gather in a dark parking lot on a hot, humid night and spend three hours asking, "Well, what do you guys want to do?" because it makes for such a crazy, zany evening. Peer pressure makes people do some strange things. Any person reading this article who has ever put on a Nehru jacket or bought a pet rock would have to admit that's true.

On the other hand, I wonder if our knee-jerk, wholesale condemnation of peer pressure isn't a bit counter-productive. Perhaps we

(Much of this material originally appeared as part of the *Hot Topics* curriculum of David C. Cook Publishing and is used here by permission.)

spend so much time blaming everything on the effects of peer pressure that some of our teenagers have begun to assume that disaster is an inevitable by-product of peer pressure. Sometimes school counselors, parents, and youth workers talk about peer pressure so much in such negative terms that teenagers feel impelled to cave into peer pressure.

Before we turn to the same old Bible passages and illustrations ("If they told you to jump into the fire, would you jump?"), it may be helpful to think a little more deeply about this problem we love to hate.

WHO ARE WE
TRYING TO KID?

Maybe we should begin by admitting that peer pressure didn't start with this generation of teenagers. If you have ever worn paisley shirts, gotten a Beatle haircut, danced the twist, swallowed a goldfish, or used a hula hoop, you know that peer pressure has been around a while.

For that matter, we should be honest enough to admit that peer pressure affects more than just teenagers. Our taste in everything from fashion to cars to lifestyle choices is almost constantly and subtly shaped by our desire to keep up with the Joneses. A recent cruise line advertised its ocean voyages by appealing to our desire to impress peers: "Holy cow, they'd never believe it, if your friends could see you now." I don't believe this ad campaign is aimed at junior highers. It's aimed at their parents!

Sometimes when we talk to teenagers about peer pressure, we talk about it as if we adults are above the fray. Let's not kid ourselves and insult our students. The desire to please our peers is common among all ages.

THE SEARCH
FOR ACCEPTANCE

When we begin to look at the effects of peer pressure in our own lives, we can perhaps appreciate more the tremendous struggles that teenagers face with peer pressure. We know from research that the most intense emotions of churched teenagers are emotions of self-hatred, the feelings that they simply do not measure up—that nobody could possibly like them the way they are.

One of the biggest errors we make in talking with students about peer pressure is underestimating their intense desire to be liked and their deep sense that, as they are, they are unlikable. Campaigns that exhort kids to *just* say no are well-intentioned, to be sure, but in the face of teenagers' struggles with self-acceptance and fear of rejection, *just* almost sounds cruel. Any discussions of peer pressure need to be laced more with compassion than sarcasm. Berating your kids for acting like chameleons just gives them one more reason to believe they are losers.

When we are talking to a fourteen-year-old kid with zits on her face, poor grades, the social life of a virus, and a figure that makes Twiggy look voluptuous, we need to realize that, from her perspective, it doesn't seem to make sense to tell them, "Just go out and be yourself."

How are teenagers coping with the issue of accepting themselves, a task made more difficult than ever with the deterioration of families and the increase of de-personalizing technologies? Canadian researcher Donald Posterski found that among students in high school, the number one source of satisfaction was a small cluster of close friends—not popularity with a lot of people, but at least some degree of intimacy with a few. What we are seeing today in the American high-school culture is a turning away from the in-crowd/out-crowd social structure of two decades ago.

Today's teenagers are more apt to conform to a small cluster of friends with whom they feel some affinity. If the cluster is made up of jocks, they will be jocks. If the kids are headbangers (kids who like their music loud and hard), they'll be headbangers. If it's computer-whizzes, they will conform to computer whizdom. Essentially, it is an effort to find some group of people with whom they feel acceptance.

As teenagers cope with the challenges of acceptance and conformity, it will be our compassion and not our ridicule that will communicate to them and nudge them in the right direction.

WHY DOES PEER
PRESSURE WORK?

Taking Posterski's findings into consideration, we get some sense of why peer pressure is so compelling for most teenagers. They taste in their conformity a lot of things for which they are hungering: acceptance (as long as they play by the unwritten rules of the group), a sense of place ("Here's a family I can count on"), and a confidence that they are measuring up to someone's expectations (a confidence that they rarely gain from home, school, the athletic field—or church, for that matter).

One of the best ways to help our students respond to peer pressure is by building in our own youth groups the kind of atmosphere that provides the same benefits they sense in more negative peer groups. Are we making our youth group a place where kids sense acceptance? Or do we invite new kids in and embarrass them the first week by asking, "Okay, now who brought their Bibles?" Do they sense that the youth group is a place where they are embraced, even with all of their weaknesses? Or do they sense an attitude that says, "Don't come here until you've cleaned up your act and dealt with your lack of faith"?

In teaching about peer pressure, we need to understand that communicating acceptance to a teenager is not the same as communicating approval of all they do. One nice thing about the average negative peer group is that you at least have some sense of what the rules are. And if you abide by those, you will be accepted. Too many times, kids walk into the church environment and are almost immediately intimidated by new rules about dress, music, and speech; rules they have never encountered and don't understand.

Listening to questions and accepting kids as they are helps to make our youth programs a place where they can sense the kind of acceptance that makes even a negative peer group feel like a good place to be. That doesn't mean that we're going to allow kids to come to youth group and act like animals. It does mean that we will understand and accept them when they act like teenagers.

IS WEIRDNESS NEXT
TO GODLINESS?

One of the main reasons that teenagers are afraid to stand against peer pressure is that they don't want to appear to be weird, gay, geeks, or Jesus freaks. Dealing with this concern will take some real sensitivity because there is tension involved here.

We would all like to believe that the best way to get people excited about Jesus is by just being a regular person—fitting in with everybody else at school, but still being a Christian. The logic here is that we aren't going to be a very good witness for Jesus if we come off looking like some kind of religious freak, so we need to work at blending in with our peers. To some extent, this is true. We probably don't do any great favor to the cause of Christ by being weird or obnoxious just for the sake of being different.

On the other hand, there's a sense in which living the Christian life with any real consistency is going to make us appear different from most of the people around us. If most people are floating downstream and we turn our boats around and start sailing upstream, then some people are going to think we're just being weird. We're not called to stand out and be weird. We are called to take a stand and be Christ-like, even if some will *think* we are weird.

We do our kids a disservice if we underplay either end of this tension. And keeping the two in balance will not be a message most of our youth will welcome. There is no easy way around this element of the gospel.

Probably the best way to show your kids that it can work— that one can be a Christian and still be likeable, attractive, and fun is by letting them see that blend in our own lives. The best way to dispel the notion that the only route to a winsome personality is by detouring around Christianity and falling in step with peers is by giving kids a living lesson through our own lives.

WHAT ABOUT
PEW PRESSURE?

As we talk to our youth about peer pressure, we are likely to overlook the fact that most kids learn a lot about conformity just by coming to church. They learn early that there is a "right" way to dress, a "right" kind of music to sing to God with, that we're not supposed to share our hurts and doubts honestly, and that we should be just Christian enough to fit in with the others in the congregation.

We need to admit that we want our students to be only partial non-conformists. We don't want them to be too radical. We want them to stand against the peer pressure that would push them to use drugs or have sex. But we want them to conform to church-oriented peer pressure. This is why we are uncomfortable when a kid turns his back on middle-class lifestyle or the American dream and decides to chuck medical school and use that expensive college degree to serve Christ in the mission field.

The reason Jesus was crucified was that he did not conform either to the non-religious people or to the religious people. His only allegiance was to the kingdom of God, and that kind of loyalty will tend to make people radical. And frankly, that makes the average church go-er perspire.

TRANSFORMATION FROM WITHIN

We quote Romans 12:2 and exhort students not to conform to the world around them, and they *do* need to hear this. But we should be careful to read the entire verse. Paul writes, "Be not conformed to this world, but *let Christ transform your mind from within*." The antidote to conformity to negative peer influence is "transformity" by Christ. Counselors and Sunday school teachers who forget this fact will go awry.

Any attempt to get teenagers to just say no will fail unless we recognize that teenagers will not say no to something unless they have, first of all, said a sincere and genuine yes to something or Someone.

CHAPTER SIX
A FAITH THAT AFFECTS THE HEART AND HEAD

It was the last night of our seven-day backpacking trip. We had shared some great experiences over the previous six days. On this last night together, we had a special time of worship around the campfire—a time that, for our group, traditionally involved a foot-washing service.

Needless to say, to wash someone's feet after they've spent six days hiking the Appalachian Trail is no picnic. Between the special emotions and the smelly feet of that last night it is no wonder that there are very few dry eyes around our campsite. I watched with anticipation as Cheryl stood and walked around the campfire in Dana's direction.

It had been a hard week for Dana. She had complained about everything: the trail was too steep ("That's why they're called mountains, Dana"), the food was lousy ("That's because this is a youthgroup function"), and her pack was too heavy (I finally agreed to carry my own tent). You name it, she griped about it. I guess that's what all of us were thinking when Cheryl knelt down to wash Dana's feet.

Dana must have been thinking about it too. Because when Cheryl began to wash her feet, I could see the tears beginning to form in her eyes. Then the tears rolling down her cheek began to glow in the light of our campfire. By the time Cheryl embraced Dana and moved back to her place in the circle, Dana was openly weeping.

At first no one said anything. No one had to. And then Dana spoke. "I have grown up in the church and I've spent these last sixteen years in a Christian household, but I don't think I've ever felt loved by anybody the way I've felt loved by you guys this week. I've been a witch to everybody, and you guys have just been patient and loving, no matter what.

"I want you all to know that just now, when Cheryl hugged me, I felt Jesus put his arms around me and hug me. It's like Jesus is saying, 'I love you, Dana, no matter what.' Thanks to all of you. I'll never forget this week or this night."

MEANWHILE,
BACK IN THE HALLWAY . . .

Those of us in youth ministry occasionally get the privilege of witnessing that kind of epiphany as we work with kids. Sometimes it happens in the regular meeting, sometimes on a work camp, and sometimes on a retreat, but it's always a wonderful experience to share in those moments when kids really feel the presence of Christ in their lives. I wouldn't for one minute devalue the importance or validity of what happened that night in Dana's life.

And yet, maybe it was cynicism—I think it was just the wisdom of experience—but no sooner had Dana made her confession and proclamation than I began wondering how I could help her translate the wonder of that mountain night in the Appalachian woods to the life she would face back home in the hallway of her high school.

How could I help her sustain the reality of God's hand on her life long after she had felt his special touch that night? I knew that she wasn't going to face this same kind of acceptance and loving patience in her everyday life. It's a rare day at the high school when someone stops in the hallway and offers to wash your feet.

Any youth minister who has had to deal with what I call Retreat Re-entry Syndrome knows that for the long haul, it will take more than warm fuzzies and neat memories to sustain students in their Christian commitment. When the heat is on and the pressure bears down, it will be God's truth and not goose bumps that helps our students stand strong in their commitment.

If we want to nurture that kind of long-term, real-life discipleship, our students need spiritual experiences *and* spiritual content. In most youth ministries, we can work on two fronts to give this kind of balanced emphasis. In the short term, we need to give more attention to the ways that we follow up on those retreat experiences. In the long term, we can make sure that we are giving our students consistent instruction and study in the Bible.

A SHORT-TERM SOLUTION: POST-RETREAT STRATEGIES

Most of us spend too much money, effort, and time on camps and retreats to allow those times to come and go without capitalizing on what God has done in the lives of our students. In my own ministry with kids, I have come across a number of strategies through the years to help our youth connect their experience on the weekend with their daily lives back home.

1. *Letters to themselves.* I have concluded a number of retreats by taking some time during our final service to have kids write a letter to themselves about what God has done in their lives while we've been away. There are a number of ways to structure this. You can encourage your youth to write this letter as if it is a letter they are writing to themselves. They should reflect on some truth that has been brought home to them over the period of the camp. It doesn't have to be some magnificent transfiguration—just one truth God has taught them over their time away.

Or I have also asked students to write these letters to themselves as if it were God writing the letter to them. "What truths does God want you to take away from this weekend? What would he want to remind you of as you go back home this afternoon?"

After the letters are written, we have the students put them in envelopes, addressed and sealed, and pass them in. We may then send them back to the students within the next week, or we may wait a few weeks, or we may send them out sporadically throughout the year. I know one youth minister who has asked her kids to let her have these letters back so that she can keep them over the years, and then at graduation, she presents this collection of personal epistles to the student.

The idea is to give students some means of capturing these truths on paper while they seem so evident and so vivid so that when they are back home in the rush of everyday life, and the retreat seems only like a memorable dream, they can be encouraged by the truth of what they know.

2. *One-to-one accountability.* Another good strategy for retreat follow-up is to allow students to choose accountability partners who

will hold them responsible for the truth they have heard over the course of the camp. On the last day of the event, structure a time in which students are given opportunity for serious conversation with a partner of their own choosing. They should be encouraged to confide in their partner at least one truth from the camp that they plan to apply in their own lives. Our goal is to help them anchor these convictions on some truth that has affected their heart, not some accountability service that has affected their heart.

There is no value in sending kids home with a resolution like, "I'm going to be a shining light in my school." That's just vague enough that accountability is virtually impossible. In each case, try to help students tie their personal decisions with some new insight or truth they have gained from the camp. (See chapter nine, "Living Out the Faith.")

Set up a pattern by which the accountability partners will covenant to contact each other once a week or more to hold them responsible for the commitment they have made. This contact can take the form of a phone call, a lunch together, or a conversation in study hall. Again, the idea is to tie the experience of the retreat into the reality of life back home—to help kids understand that even though that truth or that principle may not seem so obvious now that they are back among family and friends, it's still just as true.

A LONG-TERM STRATEGY: COMMUNICATING BIBLICAL TRUTH

I've met some youth ministers who believe the only way to know God is to experience him in some kind of dramatic way. These youth ministers usually aren't satisfied unless some of the kids foam at the mouth or see the face of Jesus on the youth-room wall. Others believe the only way to know God is through the intellect. ("Give the kids more meat!") The truth is that we nurture students best when we create an environment that affects their hearts *and* their heads.

That means that we need to stop apologizing for those mountaintop experiences we talk so much about. They are important and legitimate. But we also need to remember that our students don't live up on that mountain. And when they have to get up out of bed at 6:30 on one of those Monday-after-a-retreat mornings, we had better not be counting on their warm feelings to carry them through.

WHEN IN DROUGHT . . .

In Luke 4, just following Jesus' baptism in which the Holy Spirit descended on him like a dove (Luke 3:21, 22), we can imagine that Jesus must have been filled with a real sense of call and excitement for the ministry he was about to begin. And yet, as the stage is set for the opening act of Luke 4, we notice a very significant change. Jesus is now in the wilderness—a place of drought and desolation. And true to form, that's when Satan chooses to attack. What is remarkable about this episode is that during each of Satan's three propositions Jesus counters by using Scripture. He never once cites this incredible baptismal experience of only a few weeks earlier. It's as if Jesus knows that when under attack, it will not be experiences, but God's truth that holds the enemy at bay.

Paul was one of those kids who had a soft heart. If we had a retreat, he was guaranteed to be there, and guaranteed to have an experience with God. But when we would get back home, it was the same old pattern of half-hearted obedience and occasional whole-hearted disobedience. In a more cynical moment, I commented to one of my leaders, "Paul is a very good repenter, but very bad at repentance." I've had a lot of students like that.

They are like Tarzan, swinging from experience to experience, occasionally touching down, screaming and kicking a few natives. But they are never willing to walk with Christ in the daily jungle. Unfortunately, sooner or later, even Tarzan runs out of trees. And when kids have to give up the dizzying heights of the summer camp, the excitement and cool breezes of swinging at the Christian music festival—*that* will be the test of real-life discipleship.

Our task is not to cut out the experiences up in the tree tops, but to help kids recognize that Jesus is the vine, and that we maintain that relationship by abiding in him and allowing his truth to abide in us. "I am the vine; you are the branches. If a man remains in me and I in him, he will bear much fruit; apart from me you can do nothing . . . .If you remain in me *and my words remain in you*, ask whatever you wish, and it will be given you" (John 15:5, 7).

PROFITABLE FOR
TEACHING, REBUKING, ETC.

If we really hope to nurture our students with a faith that affects both the heart and the head, we must have an ongoing strategy that is much broader than a few periodic retreats. We must be giving our students a steady diet of truth from the Word of God. There is no other way to build into kids this component of genuine discipleship than by getting them into the Bible and getting the Bible into them.

The Psalmist puts it this way:

How can a young man keep his way pure?
By living according to your word . . .
I have hidden your word in my heart
that I might not sin against you . . .
I meditate on your precepts,
and consider your ways.
I delight in your decrees;
I will not neglect your word
    (Psalm 119:9, 11, 15, 16).

I am appalled by how many youth workers still don't do any real Bible study with their youth on a consistent weekly basis. Sometimes the excuse is that kids aren't interested. Sometimes we plead our own ignorance of Scripture. Sometimes we explain that we don't have enough volunteers to do Bible studies and do all of the other activities we feel we should be doing.

The bottom line is that we either do not understand that Bible study is essential to making disciples and that this should be our first priority, or that we are pursuing an agenda other than the one we are given in Scripture—perhaps one prescribed by denominational headquarters, or our own ego need for a large youth group. We are more interested in getting large numbers of adolescents into our church building than we are in making disciples. And if an activity such as a Bible study scares some of the kids off, we are more willing to lose the Bible than we are to lose the kids. Neither option is acceptable if we hope to have a genuine ministry of nurture.

GETTING A GAME PLAN

The vast majority of youth ministers are convinced that Bible study should be a main component of their youth program. But the confusion that I often hear voiced by both volunteers and professionals in youth ministry generally revolves around two questions: "What do I teach?" and "How do I teach it?" Let's look at each question.

Several years ago I made an observation about my own youth ministry: we were studying some of the same topics over and over again. I went back over three years worth of Bible studies and discovered that (a) we spent almost six times as much time in the New Testament as we did in the Old Testament; (b) we spent more time doing topical studies that addressed felt needs than we spent actually studying characters and themes of Scripture that might actually better address some of these felt needs; (c) our Bible study curriculum was more a reflection of my training and biases than it was a reflection of the whole counsel of God.

I decided to get together with my volunteers and talk with them about this situation. I also discussed my observations with our Pastor and some members of the Youth Committee. We came away with a curriculum of topics and studies that we wanted our youth to be exposed to prior to graduation.

We started with the basic assumption that we might have a student in our high-school program for three years. In a four-year high-school system like ours, that was a reasonable assumption. We were in a highly mobile middle to upper-middle class community, and we weren't naive to the fact that there would be students who were exposed to our group less than three years. But we decided to program to the student who would be with us for at least three years.

We then went through and discussed what kinds of topics we felt were necessary for our students by the time they graduated from high school. We tried to consider the specific needs of kids at various points during their schooling. For example, talking to seventh graders about vocation and career choice might be a bit premature. We also took into account some of the unique emphases and priorities of our congregation.

Using Larry Richards's terminology (in *Youth Ministry: Its Renewal in the Local Church*, Zondervan, 1972), we divided the topics into three categories: Bible, life, and body. The Bible category included character studies, book studies, and investigation of the basic doctrines of the Christian faith. The emphasis here was on Christian truth.

The life category included topics that dealt more with felt needs and daily lifestyle issues. The questions we investigated here were along the lines of how Bible truth could be made a part of our daily lives.

The body category was a group of topics that dealt more with our role and responsibility as members of the body of Christ. It was under this rubric that we discussed relationship issues (e.g., how do you confront a friend who appears to be wavering in his commitment? How can we show support for each other in the body of Christ? What are my spiritual gifts and how can I use them?). We also included studies of the role of the church in the world as a topical subject.

We then began to assign these topics to the years that we felt they might be most appropriate. For example, we didn't want to wait until the senior year of high school to talk about sex and dating, but neither did we plan to spend much time talking with our seventh graders about the Christian view of marriage. (As the chart on the following page reflects, we had separate Sunday school classes for 9th/10th graders, 11th graders, and 12th graders. If we had just one class for our high-school group, we would simply have recycled these topics over a three-year period, making sure that we were including a mixture of topics that would be addressing the needs of the different grades over the course of a year.)

When we had compiled our lists, we were able to set out for ourselves a three-year teaching plan that was fairly well-rounded and reflected our goals for our students.

SUNDAY SCHOOL LONG-RANGE CURRICULUM PLAN

9th/10th grade	11th grade	12th grade
BIBLE:		
Gospels	Letters of John	Book of Acts
Who is Jesus?	Romans/Corinthians	The Holy Spirit
What is a Christian?	Who is God?	Study of Nehemiah
Genesis	Study of Jeremiah	Study of Jonah
Study of David	Study of Exodus	1 Timothy, 2 Timothy
Study of Paul	Study of James	1 Thes., 2 Thes.
How to Study Bible	Prayer	Parables of Jesus
LIFE:		
Peer Pressure	Making Wise Choices	Knowing God's Will
Dealing with Temptation	Stewardship/Money	Vocation
Friendships	Drug Use/Drinking	Being Salt in World
Self-Image	Family	Christian View of Marriage
BODY:		
What is the Church?	Worship	Spiritual Gifts
Body Life	Caring for Others	Mission
Call to Service	Church Membership	Counseling Friends

Obviously, each local youth ministry is going to have different topics they want to emphasize, and different needs they feel they want to address. But this may be a good model to start with. It should be noted here that we made up a similar plan, *with some of the same topics*, for Wednesday night Bible study. That meant that students who came to Sunday school and Bible study might hear a study of some topic more than once, but we didn't see much danger with that. Also, we intentionally covered some topics (sex and dating) more than once in a three year period, using different curricula, and perhaps, coming at it from a different angle. We felt some topics needed to be repeated.

The advantage of this kind of long-range approach to curriculum planning is that it helps us to avoid two common mistakes: (1) teaching on our pet topics over and over again, and (2) falling victim to every new curriculum that comes on the market and sounds good. We can look at the topics we want to address and either purchase or develop a curriculum that is appropriate to that topic.

Having come up with a plan of topics, the next major question becomes how to communicate this biblical truth in a way that makes sense to teenagers.

CHAPTER SEVEN
THE MAGNIFICENT SEVEN LAWS OF TEACHING

In my first full-time youth-ministry position I came face to face with several sobering realizations. One of them had to do with the way I approached Bible study. I had graduated from a respectable seminary and had gained enough confidence in my training and my experience that I had begun to feel God had given me a gift of teaching. I guess that's why I was a bit surprised when I found myself teaching the Bible to a group of high-school students who didn't seem to have the gift of listening!

I had been discipled as a college student by a man who taught us regularly from the Bible. And when he taught us, apart from illustrations, he used virtually no additional teaching strategies. He never broke us into small groups. He never used drama. We never so much as twisted a pipe cleaner. He just stood up and taught us the Bible in sessions that could last up to an hour and a half. And you know what? We listened—carefully—to every word. All of us took careful notes and walked through the passages with him every step of the way.

So when I became a youth minister, I assumed that this was *the* way to do Bible study. I stood up in front of my youth group and gave them wonderful expositions of Scripture. After about four months, it dawned on me that this wasn't working very well.

To begin with, we had fewer youth in attendance every month. At first, I chalked that up to the working of conviction in the kids. But I began to realize that even the kids who stuck it out didn't seem to remember from one week to the next what I had talked about the week before. I awoke to smell the coffee, so to speak, when I said to the kids one night, "Turn with me in your Bible to John," and I looked up to see one kid actually turning the pages of his Bible, another kid thumbing through the table of contents, and the rest staring at the ceiling because they hadn't thought to bring a Bible to Bible study.

That little session in reality forced me to re-evaluate my approach to teaching the Bible to teenagers. I began to realize that when I sat eagerly in front of my mentor listening to him teach from the Bible, and taking notes, that I was being motored by a different motivation than my students on Wednesday night at youth group. If I was going to help these students grow in the Word, I was going to have to drastically change my approach to Bible teaching.

THE SEVEN LAWS OF TEACHING

It was at that point that I began to take advantage of every workshop and resource I could find that might help me broaden and deepen my approach to teaching. I became a procurement specialist for any new weaponry that might help me expand my teaching arsenal.

Some of the best counsel came from a voice that spoke from the last century. It was a classic work by educator John Milton Gregory. His principles have been described as the Seven Laws of Teaching. If we are serious about trying to nurture in our youth a faith that affects both their hearts and their heads, we would do well to heed his important words of direction. While there have been some recent books that work through each principle in more detail, we will work briefly through each of the seven laws and look at them against the background of teaching the Bible to teenagers.

LAW #1
THE LAW OF THE TEACHER

Teachers must know that which they would teach.

This seems straightforward enough and the implications are clear. If we are going to teach the Bible to teenagers, we need first of all to become ourselves students of Scripture. That doesn't mean that we need to be experts in theology and speak fluent Hebrew and Greek. It does mean that if I expect my kids to get excited about the Bible, they have to be able to see that I am excited about the Bible.

When my wife and I were going through a series of four meetings in preparation for our marriage, one conversation in the closing session almost cancelled out all that we had heard in the previous three sessions. Just as the pastor was saying how much he had enjoyed our time together, and how he was looking forward to the big day, he stopped for a moment and made a statement that gave us a jolt.

"I want to tell you folks something that may be hard for you to hear," he began, "but I want you to hear it from me before you hear it from somebody else. I intend to tell the church board tonight. You see, my wife and I have decided to get a divorce."

Now that new information did not in any way negate the fact that some of what he had already told us was true and extremely helpful. But at that point, we didn't honestly feel that we could trust very much of what he had told us about how to have a successful marriage. I suppose there was a sense in which we wanted to look beyond his announcement to us and evaluate the material on its own merit. But there was definitely a part of us that was saying "If this stuff is so helpful, why is this guy getting divorced?" That is what happens when we violate the Law of the Teacher.

I was part of a youth retreat several years ago in which the sponsoring youth minister was Dave Wintsch, a youth worker currently serving on Young Life staff up in Amherst, Massachusetts. One of my first observations of his kids was that they seemed unusually well-versed in Scripture. They were just average high-school students, but they were excited about new verses they had discovered, passages they had memorized—and I was impressed.

Over the course of time I began to meet regularly with Dave and some other youth ministers for fellowship and accountability. It wasn't long before I saw where these students had gotten their zeal for Bible study. They had caught it from Dave. He whetted their appetite for the Bible by sharing in normal conversation and in his teaching what he had tasted in the Word. That is the Law of the Teacher.

Sometimes we are deeply intent on communicating to our students the importance of Bible study, but they do not hear our lessons because they do not see that commitment lived out in our own lives. It's almost like "We interrupt this Bible study to bring you a word from our lives." And guess which message gets through the loudest to our youth.

Nobody wants to learn about navigation from the captain of the Titanic. Nobody wants to learn automobile design from the architect of the Edsel. The teacher must demonstrate that he knows that which he would teach.

LAW #2
THE LAW OF THE LEARNER

The learner must be interested or made to be interested in the truth to be learned.

"You can lead a horse to water," the old saying goes, "but you can't make him drink." Nowhere is that more evident than in a youth-group Bible study. Just teaching the Bible is no guarantee that your kids are learning the Bible. At the beginning of every Bible study, our first responsibility is to convince our students that this is material they need.

There are many ways to do this—some of them positive, and some of them not so positive. When the teacher begins the new semester in geometry by explaining that there will be five tests throughout the semester, what she is doing is giving us a reason to learn. She knows that we are not so foolish as to believe that knowing how to compute the area of a trapezoid will somehow help us in real life. She is giving us a secondary motivation for learning.

When we are teaching the Bible, we can honestly say that the material itself is the greatest reward for learning. But how do we convince our eighth grade Sunday school? That is the question!

Most of us who have flown in an airplane have heard the flight attendants give their little pre-flight pep talk about safety belts, cushions that float, exits in case of fire, and oxygen masks that drop from the ceiling. What I have noticed is that these announcements are made on every flight, and on every flight they are routinely ignored by virtually all but the newest passengers. Imagine. Here they are giving us life-saving information and we are trying to see what movie will be shown or fumbling with the barf bag.

It's not that the flight attendants don't try. They use visual aids, gestures, and in some cases, even slick videos. But from what I can observe the consensus is that this information is to be ignored. And I'm convinced it is because these friendly flight attendants have neglected the Law of the Learner.

They have neglected to gain our interest before giving us this important information. First of all, we don't feel that a seat belt or an oxygen mask will be that helpful if the plane crashes. Secondly, we don't really believe the plane is going to crash. So why listen to this gruesome presentation?

Maybe it's because I fly a lot. Maybe it's because as a youth minister, I can identify with these people. But often I have wondered how they could make this presentation a little more gripping. For instance, they might begin that nifty video with some footage of a recent crash. That would probably get our attention (and it may help to solve the overcrowded seat situation).

Or they might announce, "Ladies and gentlemen, we're glad you're flying with us today. Under your seats you will find a flotation device for use in the unlikely event of a water landing. We apologize that they are still a bit damp from our last flight . . . " Or this announcement might spark our interest: "Ladies and gentlemen, we would like to go over some of the safety features of this aircraft. We'd like to begin by pointing out the exits nearest you; but first, we do need to tell you that our right wing is on fire."

Somehow, these airline people need to make us want the information they are so anxious to give us. Otherwise, we will not learn it. That is the Law of the Learner. It is a law that is proven every week in Bible studies and Sunday school classes all over the country when youth workers stand up to give kids some teaching from the Bible that is literally life-saving information, and find themselves confronted with a nearly unanimous yawn.

How do you get adolescents to reach out for new information when they either think they know everything, or at least, think they know everything worth knowing? Somehow, we have to throw them off balance—give them new information that will make the old information no longer adequate.

Educators use the phrase "cognitive dissonance" or "cognitive disequilibrium" to describe this process of raising questions about old assumptions so that a learner is willing to listen to some new assumptions. In a sense, we are giving them new information that throws them mentally off balance into a state of cognitive (mental) disequilibrium (imbalance). It is like hearing two sounds that are out of tune with each other. You instinctively want either to adjust them so they are in harmony or turn one of them off.

Wise youth workers will understand that if they hope to give their groups some new information or insight from Scripture, it may be necessary to first cast doubts about whether their old assumptions still hold. Somehow, learners have to be thrown off balance so that their desire is to harmonize his old information with the new information, or to abandon the old information because it doesn't sound right anymore.

When I began working with teenagers, I was fired up and zealous, ready in my Bible studies to give them all the right answers. The only problem was that I had the answers, but they didn't have the questions. What I have learned is that I can sometimes teach kids more about God by asking the right questions than I can by giving the right answers. Somehow the questions get them more interested in learning a new truth. They are forced into cognitive disequilibrium, and find themselves in a situation where they need to learn.

I was once doing a Bible study with my youth group on the fruit of the Spirit, and I wanted to help them learn the difference between joy, a fruit of the spirit, and happiness, a fleeting emotional response to pleasure. Knowing my students, I sensed that this kind of dialogue would seem like unnecessary hair-splitting. One way or another, I had to figure out a way to gain their interest or they would never learn this new truth.

So we came up with a plan: Bible study began as usual that night. We spent a few minutes singing together as a group—but every song we sang had the word *happy* in it. We did all the old "happy" songs. "It's a Happy Day," "If You're Happy and You Know It," "Happiness Is To Know the Savior." It was disgusting.

Finally after about the fourth song, Thom—a volunteer—stood up and said out loud, "Duffy, doggone it, I'm sorry. I'm not trying to mess up youth group or sabotage Bible study, but I can't just keep sitting here singing all these songs about how happy I'm supposed to be, because I'm not happy."

With dropped jaws the kids listened while Thom continued, "My wife wrecked our new car yesterday; I found out I may be losing my job at the seminary; and this week I saw my summer plans pretty much wiped out. I'm sorry, maybe it's wrong. Maybe it's not very Christian. But I just don't feel happy right now." And with that, he walked out.

Now as one might expect, there were some pretty tense moments at first. Most of the kids knew that everything Thom had said was true, that it was not a good week for Thom to be singing innocuous songs about being happy. But what grew out of that awkward silence was an excellent discussion about the fact that while God does not promise us happiness, he does promise us joy. And we went on to discuss the difference between the two, with Thom quietly rejoining the group about halfway through the study.

On another occasion, we were planning to do a Bible study about prayer. And again, I was expecting my group's response to be less than enchantment. As I thought of how we could get kids interested in actually praying more consistently, it occurred to me that one of the reasons we don't pray more is because we don't really believe it's important.

If, after all, God is omniscient, then he already knows far better than I what are my needs. And if God is perfectly loving, then he already wants to meet those needs. So why do I need to pray? Our strategy on this evening was to begin by asking for prayer requests. Several kids requested prayer for various matters, and I didn't actually respond that much until finally Bill spoke up requesting prayer for an upcoming chemistry test. At that point, I asked Bill why he wanted us to pray for his chemistry test. Bill's response was predictable.

"Because if I don't do well on this test, I'm history."

"No Bill, I mean why do you want us to tell a God who knows everything that you have a chemistry test? Don't you think he knows you've got a test tomorrow?"

Bill was mildly indignant. "Yeah, yeah, of course I know that. God knows everything."

"Okay. So you're saying he knows you've got a chemistry test, but he doesn't care ... that he doesn't care that much about your chemistry tests, and unless you can get all of us to pray for you, God won't pay much attention. It's like God saying, 'Oh never mind, it's only Bill. No, wait a minute. I think I hear Duffy praying down there. Yeah, Duffy, what do you need?' "

Again Bill speaks, now with more obvious indignation. "No. I don't mean that. I know God loves all of us the same."

"Well then, Bill, I don't understand. Why should we pray for your chemistry test?"

Of course, by this time Billy's thinking, "All right, don't pray for it, you jerk!"

And at that point, I asked the others there at Bible study, "What do you guys think? Here we are sharing prayer requests. Why do we pray for each other?" It was a tough question, and some good, honest discussion followed. (One word of caution: in each of these cases I used cognitive imbalance to force students to look at some new ideas; we used it to get their attention. It was *not* the way we ended. We didn't stop the Bible study that night and say, "Okay let's close in prayer . . . well, what's the use?" I think one of the ways we can cause real harm to our students is by raising all of these questions week after week and never answering them. This is a game that seems to be especially popular among seminary-trained folks who use questions to demonstrate their superiority over kids. This is simply irresponsible.)

It was a classic case of our heeding the second law of learning: the learner must be interested or made to be interested in the truth to be learned. It was a springboard to gain the students' interest so that we could give them important information from the Bible. And we used that approach because people don't want to hear answers until they hear questions. That doesn't mean that we have to begin Bible study with a brain teaser every week. But it does mean that if we want to communicate Christian content to our kids, we should be prepared to convince them that this is information that they need.

LAW #3
THE LAW OF LANGUAGE

*Use language that is common in meaning to both
teacher and student.*

Imagine you opened a gift on Christmas morning and discovered that someone had given you an expensive new camera and that you were to faithfully record the fun and excitement around the tree. Yet when you began reading through the instructions for the option-laden camera, you saw only Japanese characters.

That is probably how the vast majority of teenagers feel when the preacher opens the Bible on Sunday morning or when we open the lesson at Bible study. They may be convinced that there is important information here, and we may have aroused their interest to listen, but all is wasted if they are not taught in a language they understand. That is what we mean by the Law of Language.

One of the speech impediments that often afflicts people who have spent a lot of time around the church is that they begin to speak in Christianese. If we are seminary or Bible college graduates, we are especially susceptible to this malady. After all, that is probably the one place in the world where you are actually affirmed for casually lapsing into Latin.

Nothing is wrong with occasionally throwing in a Greek term, or a quotation from Calvin, or even a good Christian word like *blessing*. The problem is that these words are foreign to most of the population. If we forget that, we will have a difficult time helping teenagers to study the Bible.

The longer we have been around the church, the more we tend to forget that the teenagers we work with do not traffic in churchspeak, which most of us have become comfortable with. Words like *sanctification*, *consecration*, *sin*, or even *glory* simply have no meaning in the adolescent world. They are good words—important words—but if we are trying to teach someone, we must use a language that is common in meaning to both the teacher and the student.

That means that we will have to be sensitive in how we use language in teaching the Bible to our kids. Otherwise, we will unconsciously communicate to them that this is a gift usable only by the few who know the lingo. But it also means we will need to be creative in thinking of ways to give meaning to important Christian concepts by using equivalent words that are more familiar to teenagers' ears.

For example, in 1 Timothy 6:11, Paul exhorts Timothy to pursue righteousness. That's an important idea. But if I do a Bible study with my youth group and I talk about pursuing or aiming at righteousness, most of my students would have either no idea or wrong ideas about what Paul is saying. If we don't help our students translate that word *righteousness* into language they can understand, we are, in essence, telling them to aim, but not telling them what the target is. That would discourage anybody.

I usually explain to teenagers that *righteousness* simply means *right-usefulness*. It means that I will use all that God has given me within its intended bounds — mouth, my mind, my eyes, my sense of humor, my sexuality, my abilities. Righteousness is the right-usefulness of these great gifts. Now in telling teenagers that, I may not have given them the whole story, but I have given them a working definition of what that term means. That is going to be essential if I want them to understand Paul's instruction in 1 Timothy 6. Two suggestions at this point:

1. Without trying to offend anyone, I would suggest that if we really take the Law of Language seriously, we must be intentional about getting into our students' hands a Bible translation they can understand. For those of us who love the adorned phrases of the King James Bible that may be a concept that is hard to swallow. I am always amazed at how many churches still distribute a King James Version of the Bible to children when they come through confirmation or baptism. It seems to almost suggest: "Don't try to understand it. Just admire it." If possible, see if your youth-ministry budget can provide some readable Bibles — Old and New Testaments — to the youth in your group.

2. I have found it helpful in Bible study to photocopy the text we are studying on a particular evening. By doing this, I am accomplishing several objectives. I am getting a readable translation of the text we

are studying into every teenager's hands. And I am giving all of the group a common translation of the passage so that when we study it together we are not confused by someone reading aloud from a text that is different from the others.

Another reason I hand out a copy of the passage is that the kids can use as a worksheet. One of the discoveries I made as a youth minister in the predominantly Catholic Northeast was that a lot of Catholic kids would not write in their Bibles. They felt it was somehow inappropriate, even sacrilegious. This photocopied text gave them a copy of the passage on which they could make notations, underline, and write out questions.

Inevitably, when this suggestion is made at youth-ministry workshops, someone will ask, "But aren't you discouraging kids to bring their Bibles?" Perhaps. But I think that most kids who want to bring their Bibles will bring them anyway. What I am concerned about is the young person who doesn't bring a Bible, and then has to get one out of the church library that may or may not be readable. If I want to get Bible content into that student's life, I have got to get them into a text that is written in a language they understand.

LAW #4
THE LAW OF THE LESSON

The truth to be taught must be learned through
a truth already known.

This principle is simple and it makes common sense. It is saying, in essence, that all truth is sequential. In order to understand some deeper truth, we have to understand more basic truths; and to understand those basic truths, we have to be exposed to the most elementary truths.

To put it another way: I happen at this moment to be sitting less than a mile from George Washington's headquarters at Valley Forge. If you were to decide that you wanted to visit this historic building, I could help you to get there, but I would have to lead you through a sequence of discoveries.

First, you would have to enter the state of Pennsylvania. Then you would have to enter Chester County, Pennsylvania. Then, I would have to lead you into the entrance of Valley Forge Park. And finally, I would have to lead you to the area of the park in which you could find Washington's headquarters. After we had done all that, I could show you around Washington's headquarters. Were I to skip any step in that process, I could not help you to discover this fascinating old home.

When we teach our youth the Bible, we need to remember that there is this the same kind of sequence to Christian truth. Before we can introduce them to deeper truths of Scripture, we must help our students to understand more basic truths of Scripture. And before we can help them to understand these basic truths of Scripture, we may have to walk them through some very elementary truths about God and his Word.

The mistake I often made in my early years as a youth minister was to approach my Bible study preparation as if I were preparing a Bible study for myself. I studied topics that were of interest to me, and I studied them at a level that was suited to my own spiritual walk at the time. Unfortunately, that meant that many of my early Bible studies went right over the kids' heads. I remember completing this one Bible study in which I had talked about some of the issues surrounding the gifts of the Spirit. I had done quite a bit of research into the gift of tongues and some of the more miraculous gifts. When the study was all over, one sweet sophomore girl came up and innocently commented, "That was really interesting tonight. Will you sometime tell us what the Holy Spirit is?"

LAW #5
THE LAW OF THE TEACHING PROCESS

We learn best what we discover for ourselves. The best teaching takes place when the teacher facilitates the student's self-discovery.

This is a principle all of us have already learned from life. The best way to learn not to touch a hot stove is not by having someone do a study on the essence of stoveness or principles of heat. It is by simply touching the hot stove. The Law of the Teaching Process reminds us that the best way to teach the Bible to teenagers is not by standing in front of them and talking TO them about IT. But rather, the best approach for teaching the Bible to teenagers will be to involve them WITH the Word itself, so that IT can speak TO them.

To think of this principle in another context: If you were a museum guide and you wanted to incite a love for art among your museum visitors, how would you do it? Would you meet them in the front lobby and say, "Look, since I'm the expert here and I'm afraid you'll miss something important, let me just tell you what incredible works we have in this building. We have a Rembrandt upstairs that has an awesome combination of blues and greens, and a Picasso on the third floor that seems to almost jump off the canvas. I mean, really, you wouldn't believe how magnificent some of this stuff is . . . "

Or would you meet your patrons at the front desk and say, "Okay, here's a guide to the museum. This will give you some hints about what to look for, and how to study the paintings, but I want you to look at the art for yourself. See what the artist says to you as you stare at his handiwork. Jot down your thoughts. I would love to hear your observations." In all probability, it would be this second approach that would engender a real love and appreciation for art.

And so it is in teaching Bible content to our youth groups. We can stand before them with Bible open and eyes glazed as we share with them the important and wonderful truths we have discovered in the Scripture. But the Law of the Teaching Process instructs us that the best way to help people learn the Bible will be to give the students the tools for digging, tell them where the gold is, and allow them to dig and discover for themselves.

There are a thousand and one different strategies for doing this kind of learner-centered Bible study. On any given night, one might point students to a passage of Scripture, and then invite them to investigate that passage by giving them assignments ranging from a dramatic presentation of the narrative, to a homemade slide show that depicts the flow of the story, to writing a rap about what happened in the episode.

These various investigative strategies are really nothing more than creative ways to incite your students to do inductive Bible study. It doesn't matter if the drama is an academy award winner, or if the slide show would be the envy of *National Geographic*. The goal is to get the students into the Scriptures so that God can speak to them. You are simply providing the tools to assist them as they dig into the Word.

I can recall using this learner-centered approach to Bible teaching for the first time with my high-school group about twelve years ago. I was pumped with all of these creative ideas, and excited about what kinds of incredible resources were available to help me motivate my students to study the Scripture for themselves. I wish I could write that my first attempts were marked by raucous enthusiasm and revival. But that would be a lie.

As I should have expected, my kids were skeptical of this idea at first. After all, Bible study had been much simpler when I did all the talking. Now they would actually have to engage their brains and interact with the text. And they weren't sure if it was cool to draw a coat of arms for Hezekiah and explain it to the group. They weren't completely confident about reading aloud their paraphrase of Psalm 19. It was awkward for all of us, and anyone who introduces this approach may face some reluctance at first.

But I can still remember the night when it all came together. We were doing a Bible study of Luke 19, the story of Zacchaeus. After reading through the text, the students were divided into groups of four and given various assignments. One was to write a modern-day parallel to Zacchaeus' story. Another group was to mime the Zacchaeus episode. Still another was to explain the story as if they were seeing it unfold for the first time, through the eyes of Jesus, from the perspective of Luke, or from the standpoint of the townspeople. And then the last group was to write a song about Zacchaeus to the tune of "Five Foot Two."

What a moment! John, Lisa, Jeannie, Phil, and I had worked in our group for about twenty minutes, when it was time to present our masterpiece. And it was a hit! By the time we finished that song, all of the other kids in the group broke into applause. It was one of those magic moments just made for youth-ministry books.

You could see it in John's eyes. Here was a kid who never got cheered for at the ball game on Saturday. His name was never on the honor roll at school. But here at Bible study, these people loved him! Do you think he wasn't back next week? John was thinking, "These are my people!" From that point on, our students gained a new enthusiasm and comprehension in our Bible study.

And that happened because we began to apply The Law of the Teaching Process: Students learn best what they learn themselves.

LAW #6
THE LAW OF THE LEARNING PROCESS

*The student must reproduce for himself the truth
to be learned.*

If we really want to know if our students are grasping the content that we are teaching them from Scripture, we need to know that they can reproduce that truth for themselves in their own minds, in their own words. The mistake we often make in teaching a Sunday school lesson or leading a Bible study is in thinking that students have learned the material simply because they can repeat it back to us. That is not necessarily the case.

One of the problems we run into is that by the time kids have been in Sunday school a few years they begin to learn the ropes. And one of the first rules of Sunday school survival is that if you don't know the answer to a question, just say something religious. If the teacher asks a question and you're stumped for an answer, just say, "God?" or, "Jesus?"

What kind of teacher is going to say that's a wrong answer? They are so excited that you've even remembered God's name that they are going to try to make your answer right. "Yes, okay, I guess you could say that Jesus crossed the Red Sea." Kids learn to answer us, not with what they really think, but what they think we want to hear.

Perhaps you have heard the story about a seventh-grade Sunday school teacher who had posed a simple question to his small class of seventh-grade guys: "Guys, what is gray and furry and stores up nuts for the winter?" Well, anyone who has ever taught seventh-grade Sunday school knows what happened next. Eight heads bowed, sixteen pairs of eyes immediately began to stare at the floor. Complete silence. Where only moments ago before class began there was laughter and talking and spontaneity, now there was all the vitality of a cemetery.

The teacher posed his question again: "Come on, guys. What's gray and furry and stores up nuts for the winter?" Again, he was met with silence. Finally, he queried the group a third time. "Hey guys, don't be stupid. What's gray and furry and stores up nuts for the winter and has a long bushy tail?"

At this point, Jimmy nudged little Freddy. Freddy turned red as a beet, and the teacher said, "Okay Freddy, you tell us. What is gray and furry and stores up nuts for the winter?" Freddy, nervous and embarrassed, answered in a small, apologetic voice, "Well, the answer is Jesus—but it sure sounds like a squirrel to me."

So many times we confuse repetition with realization. The Law of the Learning Process reminds us that just because a student can repeat the right words doesn't mean that they actually comprehend what we've been teaching. We need to probe students' understanding of a truth by asking them to restate it in their own words, apply it to their everyday world and talk about how they would explain it to a friend. Only if they can reproduce the truth in these ways can we be sure that the truth has been learned.

LAW #7
THE LAW OF REVIEW AND APPLICATION

The best way to build for retention of a truth that has been learned is through review and application.

I have read that most people have to hear something eight times before they will actually remember it. Whether that piece of trivia is accurate or not, all of us know that it isn't easy to get a message through and make it stick. One study showed that of every 100 people who actually watch a television commercial, only thirty genuinely pay attention to its content, and of that number, only half—*fifteen*—understand the content, and of that number, only five people actually retain the content of the commercial in their active memory twenty-four hours later.

If that's the best Coca-Cola and McDonald's can do, what chance do we have with our forty-five minutes of Bible study once or twice a week? It isn't easy. We need to heed very carefully the point of The Law of Review and Application. Our best insurance that students will not only hear our Bible teaching, but retain the content in their active memory beyond Sunday lunch, is to give them heavy doses of review and application.

Review is simple enough. That means that we continue to give students a chance to see this content, in different forms and worded and embodied in different characters and principles, but driven home over and over again. If it is worth hearing once, it's worth hearing twice. I am convinced that one of the reasons my colleague and good friend Tony Campolo has made such an impact with his sermon, "It's Friday, but Sunday's Comin' " is that he took one theme and played it over and over again.

During my youth-ministry years in Wilmore, Kentucky, I had the good fortune to work with David Seamands as my Senior Pastor. I quickly discovered the genius of David's preaching that transformed so many people over the years. He took one theme, God's grace, and every week he preached that theme one way or another. He used hundreds of different passages, but somehow he laced it all back to the grace of God. And people heard that message. They retained that content. And lives were changed.

But if repetition is important, application is even more important. A truth that is not applied to the everyday lives of our youth is almost certainly going to be forgotten. Theirs is a world in which there is simply too much going on to be concerned about some theological trivia that seems unconnected to the everyday world. When you're working your way through puberty, establishing identity, understanding sexuality, and going to school, gaining Bible information strictly for the sake of information is probably a luxury you can't afford. If we want our students to retain the content we teach from Scripture, we need to help them understand how it applies to where they live.

When I began doing youth ministry, I was working under the assumption that if I could change the kids' minds, I could change the kids' actions. I still believe that is true. But now I understand from experience and from more recent psychological research that I had it backwards. The way to impact a person's thinking is to impact his or her actions. It is actions that shape our thinking and not thinking that shapes our actions.

Anyone who has ever taken a mission trip with their youth group has probably observed this principle at work in their group. Before the trip you could talk to your youth about missions until you were hoarse. But the group continued to rank mission work right up there on the excitement scale with oral surgery and long talks with Dad about puberty. Then you take them to Tijuana or Port-au-Prince for a week, and half of those in the group decide they are going to be missionaries.

The best way to help a student learn to trust God is not simply by doing a Bible study on trusting God, but by challenging the student to think of some specific areas in his life in which he can trust God, and some specific steps that they will take on the basis of that trust. Then we help the student explore a specific way that he can apply the biblical truth he has been taught.

If our basic assumption is that God says what he says because it is truth, then we can have complete confidence that every time our students act on that truth, the Word will verify itself. Every time students apply that truth, they review it and renew it in their minds.

One practical discipline that can keep us honest in this area is what I call *anchoring*. Whenever I complete a Bible study, I want to make sure there is some truth in that study or talk that students can anchor back into one of the five spheres of their everyday lives: social (friends of the same sex and friends of the opposite sex), school, family, interior life (personal dreams, hopes, fears, concerns), and kingdom (local church, youth group, and body of Christ as a whole). Teenagers walk into and out of each of these five spheres of life on almost a daily basis. If we can help them to see how a new spiritual truth will impact one or more of these areas, we greatly increase our chances of not just teaching the Bible, but of helping people to learn the Bible.

Psychology Today published a remarkable incident concerning the life and death of the Prince of Granada, an heir to the Spanish crown. Centuries ago the Prince was sentenced for life to solitary confinement in Madrid's ancient prison, the Place of Skulls. Apparently, the authorities feared he might aspire to the throne. During his imprisonment he was given one book to read—the Bible.

Over the course of the years, the Prince of Granada apparently read the Bible hundreds of times and read it with painstaking care. But when he died after thirty-three years of imprisonment, and the authorities began going through his cell after his burial, what they found was striking.

All over the walls of his cell, they found that he had etched in the soft stone notations such as these:

The eighth verse of the 97th Psalm is the middle verse of the Bible; Ezra 7:21 contains all the letters of the alphabet except the letter "J";

The ninth verse of the eighth chapter of Esther is the longest; No word or name of more than six syllables can be found in the Bible.

As O'Dell points out, it is incredible that this man spent more than thirty years carefully studying this one book that has been described even by its critics as one of the most amazing pieces of literature ever written, and all he gleaned from his study was a few isolated pieces of Bible trivia (Scott O'Dell, "David: An Adventure With Memory and Words," *Psychology Today*, January 1968).

The Prince is certainly not the only one to walk away from the Bible empty-handed and empty-headed. Our students face the same danger.If we are intent on helping our students develop a faith that affects their heads and their hearts we must help them review and apply the truths we teach from Scripture. Otherwise, we too will be faced with teenagers who have gone through years of exposure to the Bible, and have walked away from our youth ministries with little more than Bible trivia.

CHAPTER EIGHT

MAKING THE MAGNIFICENT SEVEN WORK FOR YOU

TEACHING THE BIBLE: APPLYING THE SEVEN LAWS

Having reviewed these seven principles of teaching, the obvious question is, "How does it all work out in a Bible study or a Sunday school lesson? How can I put together a lesson that takes seriously these seven laws?"

The diagram below suggests a possible format:

BIBLE STUDY FUNNEL

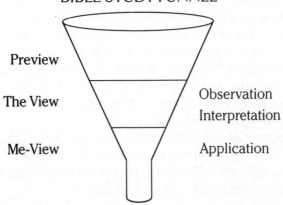

Preview

The View — Observation / Interpretation

Me-View — Application

This diagram illustrates that building a Bible study from scratch should involve four elements of focus. Depending on the curriculum, these stages may be called anything from "Hook, Book, Look, and Took" to "Approach, Bible Exploration, Life Exploration, Conclusion." Essentially the funnel reminds us that there are four important elements of effective Bible study: grabbing the student's interest, using that interest to motivate the student to study the Scripture, helping the student understand and interpret what has been read, and then helping the students apply the spiritual truth to their lives.

Each stage is critical to the whole. And each stage involves use of various learner-centered Bible learning activities.

PREVIEW

This portion of the Bible study is simply designed to incite the student's interest in the truth to be learned. This may involve a case study, a story, a question, a drama, or even a game of some type. The basic assumption is that when our kids come to Bible study or Sunday school, some have an interest in the topic for study, but the majority are not walking in with their hands outstretched saying, "Fill my cup, I lift it up."

We will have to earn their ear. We will have to realize that when they walk into that Bible study, they are coming from a myriad of life situations and mindsets. Billy has just been making out with Sally in the church parking lot. Susie came early because she wanted to find out if Steve and Cindy are going steady. Bob staggers in with a smile on his face but a stake in his heart because tonight at dinner his parents announced they will be getting a divorce. Michelle floats into the room because she found out this afternoon that she made cheerleader. Our assignment is to bring all of these folks from their various worlds to the Word of God.

That means that our Bible study must be broad enough at the outset to have the potential of grabbing the interest of the uninterested and distracted. This is the Law of the Learner applied. I refer to this portion of the study as the PREVIEW.

THE VIEW

This is the segment of the Bible study when, now that we have the student's attention, we direct it to the Bible. That is why we have done the PREVIEW—so that we could direct the student's attention to THE

VIEW. I grew up in a Sunday school class where the teachers seemed to take great pains to get our attention but then never could bring themselves to risk losing our attention by directing it to the Scripture. That amounted to a lot of wasted Sunday mornings.

If all we have is spectacular PREVIEWS and never actually help the students get into the passage, we will soon be ignored. It would be as if we shouted to a group of people, "Hey! Hey! Over here! Look!" And then when we had their attention, we smiled and said, "Thanks." It wouldn't be long before people ceased to take us seriously.

This THE-VIEW portion of the Bible study brings with it two tasks: Observation and Interpretation. We want to use various Bible Learning Activities (BLAS) to help the students examine what the text says. That's observation. It has to do with the setting, the characters involved, the action that takes place, the subject of the teaching—the who, what, when, and where questions.

Then using learner-centered strategies, we want to help students ask, "What does the text mean?" That's interpretation. I can read in Luke 19:10 that Jesus described Zacchaeus as "lost." But it will take some interpretation to understand why he said that and what he meant by it.

It is not enough simply to read that I must love my neighbor. I need to consider what it means to love my neighbor and I've got to ask who my neighbor is. It would probably be in this part of the Bible study that we would apply the principles of The Law of the Learning Process. We wouldn't want to leave this section of the study until the students are able to describe in their own words the message of the passage. That is the work of Interpretation.

ME-VIEW

In this final section of the study then, we are ready to move beyond the question of what the passage says, and what the passage means, to the question, "What does it mean to me?" At this point we will guide our students to use this passage as a probe to see where they might have weaknesses with which to deal, or promises to apply, or sins to confess.

During the ME-VIEW section of the Bible study, we take what we have read and apply it to our own lives and to the lives of our students. From what we know of the Law of Review and Application, this portion of the study is critical. I suggest that youth ministers ask themselves at the beginning of every Sunday school lesson or Bible study: "If my students actually take me seriously in this Bible study [they might, you know], what will be different about their lives when they leave this room?" If youth ministers cannot answer this question, they need not waste their time or the kids' time on the study.

God did not give us his Word for information. He gave it for transformation. Any Bible study that stops short of helping youth apply God's Word to their lives just gives teenagers one more reason to believe the Bible isn't worth studying because it doesn't really matter anyway.

WHAT DOES IT
LOOK LIKE?

Before we close out this chapter, consider the following example of a Bible study that follows the basic format we've suggested above and adheres to the Seven Laws of Learning. It is material I prepared a few years ago for a Sunday school elective published by the United Methodist Church ("Senior High Sunday School," Winter Quarter, 1988, United Methodist Publishing House).

I am including here background material and instructions that were intended for the teacher. With a minimal amount of creativity and a good clip art book (see *Youth Specialties Clip Art Book*, Youth Specialties), a sharp youth worker could take this material and prepare some creative student handouts to accompany this study.

JEREMIAH'S CALL

Key Verse
The word of the Lord came to me, saying,
"Before I formed you in the womb I knew you,
and before you were born I set you apart;

I appointed you as a prophet to the nations."
Jeremiah 1:4–5.

Bible Lesson
Jeremiah 1:4–10, 17–19

In this dreary situation, Jeremiah was called to bring an unpopular word of judgment and, later, what must have sounded like an insane promise of future blessing (chapters 23, 30, 33).

Begin this lesson by asking students to respond to this question: "What assignment or task have you ever been asked to do that really got you scared?" Simply list the situations on a large sheet of paper or a blackboard so that all of your students can see them. Then allow them to list the situations in order of the fear they invoke.

Or have your students respond to this little survey about "Missions Impossible."

MISSIONS IMPOSSIBLE SURVEY

Every now and then, we're called on to do a job that we feel completely unprepared for. Look at the list below and rank the activities in the order of those that would put you in the most dread and fear. Rank the most fearful beginning with a number one:

_____ singing in front of a school assembly—by yourself

_____ changing a diaper

_____ giving a sermon

_____ asking someone out on a date

_____ dueling with Darth Vadar

_____ asking Darth Vadar out on a date

_____ changing Darth Vadar's diapers

The idea is not to take this warm-up seriously. Your goal is simply to put your students in touch with feelings of insufficiency and despair that come along with trying to carry out a mission for which they feel incapable.

"If it's you calling, God, I think you may have the wrong number."

Jeremiah was a young man when he was called by God to give a rather grim message to his people in the nation of Israel. In Jeremiah 2:19, you begin to get the drift of God's message through Jeremiah and it wasn't exactly pleasant:

> "Your wickedness will punish you; your backsliding will rebuke you. Consider then and realize how evil and bitter it is for you when you forsake the Lord your God and have no awe of me, declares the Lord, the Lord Almighty."

This is not the sort of stuff you want written in your yearbook.

And yet God's call to Jeremiah was clear. Read Jeremiah 1:4–10. What emotions do you suppose Jeremiah must have been feeling in response to God's call on his life? Imagine that you are Jeremiah and that you are recording your thoughts in your diary one night as you listen to the radio up in your room. What would you write?

Maybe one of the reasons that Jeremiah seemed so uptight about God's call is that he just didn't feel he measured up to the stereotype of your normal everyday prophet. In a small group of no more than three, draw up a want ad entitled, "Prophet needed—see God."

Allow some of the groups to share their want ads. Then ask, "What does it take to make a good prophet? How would Jeremiah measure up with the prophetic position in your want ad?"

A Prophet-Making Venture

What makes Jeremiah's call so exciting is that God never denied any of Jeremiah's excuses. He only shifted the focus from Jeremiah's weaknesses to God's strengths. Reading through the passage again, list below Jeremiah's excuses about why God couldn't use him, and list God's replies about how Jeremiah *could* be used.

Jeremiah's Doubts	God's Replies

If you had been Jeremiah, what would have encouraged you most about God's replies? Why?

The Call of Yuandiah (you and I)

As scary as it is, and as hard as it is for some of us to believe, God wants to call each of us into his service just as he did Jeremiah. It's kind of tough to see yourself as a prophet to the nations when you can't even spell Euphrates, and when your name is Bill or Sally, not Jeremiah or Zedekiah. But how can *you* be a prophet, a spokesperson for God in your school? Come up with some ideas in your small group and list them.

What excuses are you giving right now in an effort to put God's call on hold? *God's Call, and Putting Him on Hold*

Imagine that God is writing you a letter today to encourage you to follow through on his calling in your life. Write below the letter that he would write.

Dear (You):

Love, God

CHAPTER NINE
LIVING OUT THE FAITH

Imagine: You're driving some kids in your youth group to a ball game across town. You overhear a conversation between two of your sharpest kids who are thanking each other for the dubious help they gave each other during the chemistry exam.

Or one of your small group leaders comes to your office to report that she is pregnant.

Or you find out that one of your key guys has deceived his parents into thinking that he was at a discipleship meeting so that he could go to a friend's party.

Have you ever had that sinking feeling that one of the toughest parts of Christian nurture is not getting kids to BECOME Christians, but getting them to BE the Christians they've become?

What is so scary about the situations mentioned above is not just that these are Christian kids doing wrong, but in some cases these Christian kids don't actually realize or believe that they are doing wrong. One of the major aspects of Christian nurture is to help the students in our youth ministry integrate their faith and their everyday life on a consistent basis. In short, we want to help them walk their talk.

James addressed this same concern in his letter to the Hebrew Christians.

Do not merely listen to the word, and so deceive yourselves. Do what it says. Anyone who listens to the word but does not do what it says is like a man who looks at his face in a mirror and, after looking at himself, goes away and immediately forgets what he looks like. But the man who looks intently into the perfect law that gives freedom, and continues to do this, not forgetting what he has heard, but doing it—he will be blessed in what he does (James 1:22–25).

What good is it, my brothers, if a man [or youth] claims to have faith but has no deeds? Can such faith save him? Suppose a brother or a sister is without clothes and daily food. If one of you says to him, "Go, I wish you well; keep warm and well fed," but does nothing about his physical needs, what good is it? In the same way, faith by itself, if it is not accompanied by action, is dead (James 2:14–17).

WHY THE FAITH ISN'T WORKING

There are a number of reasons why the youth in our groups may be good talkers but bad walkers when it comes to their Christian life. Of course, the problem of our sinfulness would factor right up there as one of the leading causes. After all, this kind of flimsy obedience and cheap faith was not invented by the current generation of teenagers.

On the other hand, there are some mitigating factors that might make the issue even more cloudy for today's youth. As youth workers committed to helping nurture in teenagers a faith that works, we need to be aware of some of these factors.

1. Biblical Illiteracy

A few years ago, E. D. Hirsch, Jr. wrote a book that stirred quite a bit of discussion among educators and cultural observers around the country. His book *Cultural Literacy: What Every American Needs To Know* (Houghton Mifflin, 1987) argued that the vast majority of today's high-school graduates are walking away from high school with a diploma that essentially means very little. Hirsch cited the lack of familiarity with the great classics of literature, a limited knowledge of history, and almost complete ignorance in matters of geography.

One study showed that more than fifty percent of American high-school students thought Columbus discovered America sometime during the 1700s. Another study observed the surprisingly high number of American college students who could not find Iran, Colombia or Miami on a map of the world. Hirsch argues that our schools are producing graduates who are culturally illiterate.

While that certainly should concern us, there is a problem that should perhaps concern us even more: biblical illiteracy. We have a growing number of students who have virtually no notion of what the Bible teaches. Students who are well-rounded in other areas of educational study are ignorant about the God of Israel, the story of Moses, or even the life and teachings of Jesus. This is not just a phenomenon outside the church. There is growing biblical illiteracy inside the church.

In a youth-ministry internship I served while in seminary, I was astounded how many of the teenagers in the group were absolutely ignorant about the Bible. Wakefield was a middle- to upper-middle-class community with families who, I am quite sure, wanted their children well-educated. Some of them were taking advanced courses in school. They were intelligent students. But many of them had grown up in this church in suburban Boston and had never learned something as simple as reading a biblical reference (e.g., John 3:16). Quite literally, they did not understand that the first word is the name of the book of the Bible, then comes the chapter, and then the verses.

A Gallup Poll shows that Christian teenagers are inconsistent in Bible reading, could rarely cite all of the Ten Commandments, and could only occasionally recall the names of all four of the Gospels. If we are inclined to doubt this data, all we have to do is survey our own youth group. How many of the kids in your youth group know where in the Bible to find this verse: "God helps those who help themselves"?

That means that our youth ministries are filled with teenagers who may be computer-literate, but who know nothing about the call of discipleship or Jesus' teaching in the Sermon on the Mount. They have never wrestled with the high calling of the New Testament or the expectations of the Holy God of the Old Testament. When it comes to the Bible, they are simply illiterate. It is no wonder that their understanding of obedience is shallow.

2. *Superficiality*

If our students lack genuine understanding of the biblical landscape, we shouldn't be surprised that their understanding of the Christian life is somewhat superficial. Because they have not witnessed the courage of an Isaiah, the boldness of a Stephen, or the compassion of a Hosea, they lack a sense of perspective on the Christian life.

It is easy to say yes when you don't really understand what sort of no's that yes will entail. I can recall the feeling of awe that I felt on my wedding day more than sixteen years ago when I began to realize the depth of the commitment I was making. I had seen this marriage commitment up close in the lives of my own parents. I knew what it meant. At least to some degree, I was marriage-literate. And that sense of understanding made me all the more aware that saying yes to this woman meant saying no to other things.

Because our youth have virtually no sense of biblical landscape, and because they have grown up in a culture that thinks of commitment as any decision that lasts beyond sundown, our teens are making superficial commitments to Jesus Christ. They are quite willing to say yes to Jesus, but they do not understand that that means saying no to some things that are "not Jesus," so to speak.

My friend Mike was recently speaking at a ski retreat where he saw this problem illustrated clearly. The retreat was held in a resort hotel. Just before the meeting one night, a group of guys told Mike that they were really enjoying the sessions and getting a lot out of his talks, but wondered if he could finish up a little bit early that night so that they could get downstairs to the hotel lobby by nine c'clock? Mike suggested they clear the schedule change with their youth leader and didn't think much more about it.

When the meeting concluded shortly after nine that night, these guys flew past Mike out the door of the meeting room toward the hotel lobby. Trying to be friendly, Mike said that he was sorry that the schedule change hadn't worked out, and the four lobbyists assured Mike it was no problem. Besides, they said, they really liked the sermon.

The boys' youth leader overheard the conversation and asked Mike what it was about. Mike explained, adding that he had suggested the four guys talk to the youth leader.

"They did ask," the leader said, "and I told them no. Do you know why they wanted to get downstairs by nine tonight? Tonight in the lobby the hotel is sponsoring a lingerie fashion show that those guys didn't want to miss."

We need to understand that it is possible for our students to really enjoy our talks, really get a lot out of them—and still see no problem with walking out of that Bible study and into a living lingerie show that they'd also really enjoy and get a lot out of.

Sad to say, that is partially our fault. We have been more eager for kids to say yes to Jesus than for them to say no to other things.

Some time ago I was attending a large denominational youth gathering that concluded with an outdoor worship service. All of the bishops and church leaders were there with robes, sashes, vestments—the works.

The closing portion of the service involved the playing of a song from the Woodstock soundtrack (an outdated choice, I thought, but one that I assumed church leaders used to let the youth know how hip they were). The song ended, but the soundtrack continued—and the kids who only moments before had recited the liturgy flowed smoothly with Country Joe and the Fish into his celebrated f---cheer. There was no sense of outrage, no sense of incongruency. No one killed the tape. The church leaders seemed to be resigned that kids will be kids.

3. *Lack of Authentic Models*

Equally confusing for students who are trying to understand how the Christian life is played out on the stage of everyday life is the lack of authentic models for them to look to. A professional baseball player is outspoken about his faith and is invited to give his testimony at youth gatherings throughout southern California. Then comes the announcement that this outspoken Christian has been having an affair with two different women, while seriously dating a third whom he plans to make his second wife.

When the two women sue for child support for the babies he has fathered, the outspoken Christian holds a press conference to announce that "as a Christian" he will "do the right thing" and be responsible for the two children he has fathered. Teenagers are not the only ones bewildered by that kind of commitment.

With the growing amount of publicity given to the moral failures of various well-known Christians, it is increasingly difficult for teenagers to take seriously the gospel's call for righteous living. Teenagers grow cynical because everybody preaches that kind of commitment, but nobody lives it out.

George, a youth-ministry colleague, was recently approached by one of his key volunteers who announced that she was pregnant. Since this woman had gotten married only two weeks before, the rumors began to fly. While the volunteer told George that she and her fiancé had only slept together once prior to their marriage, the message to the kids in the youth group was loud and clear. As is so often the case, our actions speak much louder than our words.

When she and her husband explained to the youth group why they would be taking a leave of absence from their youth-group involvement, George observed that the disillusionment was obvious. One seventh grader who had just been led by the couple through a series on Christian sexuality, spoke to this woman out of an obvious sense of disappointment. "How could you be teaching us to say no to sex before marriage when you were having sex with your boyfriend the whole time?" Good question.

4. *Wrong Views of God*

Another factor that has probably contributed to the gap between our students' commitment to Christ and their everyday lifestyle is their misunderstanding of the nature of God. A study of Luke 19:11–27 will show that the unfaithful servant acted as he did because he had a wrong concept of God. "I was afraid of you, because you are a hard man" (Luke 19:21).

In youth ministry today we are largely working with teenagers who are laboring under one of two false assumptions. The first is that God is a hard man (Luke 19:21), a God whom we fear and from whom we hide. This is the Santa Claus God, who's making the list, checking it twice, and is gonna find out who's naughty or nice. Needless to say, just as with Santa Claus, this view of God doesn't inspire much year-round genuine obedience.

Emphasizing this Santa Claus view of God has been the mistake of many in youth ministry. David Seamands, professor of pastoral ministry at Asbury Theological Seminary, has commented that the majority of people he sees in counseling are people who have come out of the holiness tradition which taught them that God was a legalistic sheriff who wanted to corral them instead of a loving shepherd who wanted to care for them. He helps them to rebuild a balanced view of God as the Father of grace.

The second false view of God that pervades the teenage culture is the George Burns God—a cigar-smoking old geezer whose motto is "Every now and then, we all want to have a good time, so let's not be so puritanical." But that view of God, made popular in recent movies, depicts God, as C.S. Lewis pointed out, not as a father in heaven, so much as a grandfather in heaven, a senile old gentleman whose major concern at the end of the day is that everyone had a good time.

This view of God is equally alive and well in youth ministries around the country. Betraying the biblical portrait of God as holy, righteous, and wrathful towards disobedience, a youth minister explained away his kids' dilemma about pre-marital sex by pointing out that "the bottom line is not what is right or wrong, but what is right for you." Unfortunately, that insight never came from Scripture.

5. *Lack of Practical Teaching*

Mary was one of those teenagers who had made a commitment to Christ, and wanted sincerely to abide by that commitment. But her problem was that she really didn't know how. She would go forward during the semi-annual church-wide renewal services and every year her conviction was the same: "I'm just not living the way God wants me to. I can't explain it. I want to live for Christ, but I just keep blowing it."

Inevitably, some well-meaning preacher or youth speaker would counsel Mary to *really* turn her life over to Christ. So Mary would *really* turn her life over to Christ. Then after several months, she would turn back again, discouraged and defeated because she still wasn't perfect. Another trip to the altar, and another exhortation to *REALLY* turn her life over to Christ. Then that would work out for a few months until she once again felt discouraged, and there would be another trip to the altar and another exhortation, and on it went.

What was missing in Mary's Christian life was not inspiration, but information. She didn't need to make another trip to the altar. She needed someone to give her some plain language about how she could practically live out her faith. She didn't need nagging. She needed practical teaching.

I'm convinced that Mary's situation is not unusual. Our kids hear us teaching in vague terms about loving our neighbors, but they aren't sure what that means in practical terms. How do I love my neighbor when my neighbor asks for my answer on the English exam? How do I love my neighbor when he asks me to lie for him when his mother calls to verify where he was last night? How do I love my neighbor when my neighbor is using drugs and he insists that he doesn't need help to get clean?

One of the reasons that our youth do not live out their faith on a consistent basis is that they do not have enough practical teaching about how to do that. We need to give our students not only the content of Scripture, but we need to help them know how that truth practically impacts daily life.

FACING AND EMBRACING THE TRUTH

If we are going to help teenagers learn how to integrate their faith and their everyday lives, we need to think about how we learn and apply any new information. For that reason, we want to draw from the work of former Brandeiss University psychologist, Abraham Maslow. So far as we know, Maslow never led a junior-high Bible study or spoke at a lock-in, but his insights into the Four Levels of Learning are helpful for those of us in youth ministry.

Level One: Unconscious Incompetence

Before teenagers ever come in contact with a new Christian truth, they are in the first level of learning, described by Maslow as Unconscious Incompetence. In other words, teenagers at this stage of learning know so little about a new truth that they don't even know what they don't know! They are so unaware at this stage, that they are unaware of their ignorance. They are unconscious of their incompetence.

About a year ago, I was speaking at a post-Christmas retreat for high-school students from prep schools all over the northeast. It was a rare and exciting opportunity to speak to kids who were very well-educated in secular matters, well-traveled, and articulate, but, in some cases, had never been inside a church or a Christian meeting of any kind. This was their first encounter with Christian truth.

After I had finished speaking one night, I was approached by one of the students, a young man with a ready smile and an open, inquisitive face. He affirmed me in an unorthodox way: "Hell, Duffy, I just want you to know that's the best damn sermon I've ever heard!" He shook my hand and walked out of the room.

I stood there reflecting that this high-school kid had just introduced me to something new: I had never completed a talk and had someone express their appreciation like that. At first I was sort of shocked. I wasn't sure what to say. I felt like I should probably respond with a slap on the back and say, "Hell, thanks, that's mighty damn kind of you!" I almost laughed as I thought of it.

But what was so refreshing about this young man's comment is that it was entirely authentic. He wasn't trying to be crude or profane. He honestly didn't know that these are not the usual compliments extended to Christian speakers. This was all so new to him that he didn't even know what he didn't know. He was unconsciously incompetent.

During my seminary years in Boston, I worked with a number of teenagers who had never heard the most basic elements of the gospel, had never heard any kind of Christian teaching. They thought they had. They had heard teachers, friends, or parents make comments based on stereotypes and had accepted those stereotypes as true. But they didn't even realize how much they didn't know.

Some of the kids in our youth groups do not integrate Christian truth into their daily lives because they are simply unaware and ignorant of what God tells us to do. A youth minister friend of mine out in California was explaining to his group what the Bible says about sexual purity inside and outside of marriage. One of his kids suddenly interrupted with all the shock of a Eureka experience: "You mean no sex at all before marriage? Really? Do you think that would work?" It was as if this kid had just discovered sliced bread.

On other occasions, unconscious incompetence will leave kids less open to discovery. Their attitude will be manifest in a kind of arrogance that can be a bit intimidating to youth workers. They appear to have it all together. They seem to have all the answers.

But that may just be because they don't know all the questions. If you don't know that a tornado is looming in the distance, you are going to appear indifferent when someone attempts to explain tornado-safety precautions. That's not because you know so much. It's because you know so little. We need to be careful not to be put off or intimidated by that attitude.

On the other hand, I often find it refreshing to meet students who are genuinely at the earliest level of learning. My opinion is that if they haven't learned anything, then, at least, they haven't already learned some wrong things. I appreciate the honesty and freshness of a teenager who is unconsciously incompetent.

These teenagers haven't learned some of the Christian games that we play to cloak our feelings and questions. They just come right out with it. Sometimes these kids are more open to instruction about how Christ impacts our lives than the kids who have sat through fifteen years of Sunday school.

Level Two: Conscious Incompetence

Maslow's second level of learning can be applied to kids who are actually hungry to learn. They don't know how a Christian should respond in a given situation or to a given situation, but at least they KNOW that they don't know. That's a step up from level one. We are apt to find more teachability here.

The Bible studies we do in front of teenagers on a weekly basis may be well-received. The kids (most of them) may listen and participate in the discussion. But the best teaching happens when students are concerned about some problem with their parents or with their girlfriend or boyfriend and they come and ask our counsel. That is when the teaching opportunity is ripe, because at this point, the students have become conscious of their incompetence.

This is the attitude that is so invigorating for those who do seminars around the country for youth workers. Early in the meeting people walk into the workshop worn and battle-weary. They sit in front ready to listen, ready to learn. Perhaps a year or so ago, when they signed on as volunteers they were thinking, "Hey, how difficult can it be? I was a teenager once. I'm pretty cool. I can pull this off."

But now a year later, they have a different attitude. These folks are saying, "Okay, now, can we go over a few things? Is it, like, you know, normal for the kids to set fire to your automobile?" It's a whole different attitude.

In fact, I see the difference sometimes when I walk into my youth-ministry classes at Eastern College. I have just gotten back from doing a seminar for hungry youth workers, who know what they don't know. Then, I give these young college students this very same information about how youth ministry works. But the problem is, of course, they aren't out there on the front lines. They still have the luxury of sitting in a classroom out of the line of fire. And their attitude is often, "Will this be on the test?"

Level Three: Conscious Competence

I was playing racquetball with a teenager a few weeks ago, and not doing too badly for an old guy. In fact, if I may say so, I was devastating this young buck—all in the interest of ministry, of course. He was a growing Christian and it gave us a chance to spend time together and strengthen our growing relationship. I'm sure he still felt a bit uncomfortable about spending time with this adult minister-professor type, but he was relaxing.

At least he seemed to be relaxing, until he tripped over his own legs trying to scramble across court. Instinctively, he set sail a fleet of expletives and curse words that he hadn't picked up in Bible study. Immediately, as if he'd realized his mistake, he turned to me and apologized. "Sorry. Old habit, you know . . . "

What my young friend demonstrated was actually very encouraging to me. He was showing me that he was moving into a new level of awareness about how he could work out his faith on a daily basis. My friend was conscious of what he should do as a Christian, and desired to do it, but it was not his natural reaction. Maslow describes this level of learning as Conscious Competence.

Our youth, at this stage, know how they should respond as Christians. They know enough now to be able to integrate their faith with their daily behavior. But they are not so comfortable with this new faith, or their new commitment to obedience, that this integration is unconscious. It is, rather, conscious competence.

I remember as a young junior higher the first occasion that I kissed a girl. I didn't know much about kissing a girl. My attitude was a mixture of rookie nervousness and intense willingness to learn. I had seen examples of this activity in movies and was intrigued. I had talked to my expert friends in eighth grade, but I still felt uneasy. Then came that warm spring evening when I began to implement the truth I had been taught.

It was a near disaster. I was so scared I would do something wrong—and noticeably wrong—that romance or passion was the last thing on my mind. There was no pleasure. Only intense concentration. As she moved closer, I could hear the sirens and bells, but they were warning sounds: "Mayday, Mayday, brace for contact." It was scary. Later on I became more proficient at this activity, and found it became easy, even pleasurable. But that initial awkwardness and sense of foreboding is characteristic of conscious competence.

Christian teenagers who are attempting to integrate their faith with their everyday life probably feel the very same kind of discomfort in trying to live out the Christian life. It's new. It's strange. They can respond to their daily situations as a Christian, but it doesn't come easily.

The Apostle Paul speaks of the Christian life as a process of putting off the old life and putting on the new clothes of a life in Christ. "Clothe yourselves," he explains in Colossians 3:12. If we can visualize that process of putting off and putting on, we have a sense of how awkward it can be for teenagers to begin to try to live out their Christian faith. It's like wearing a new pair of shoes. It's like taking off an old, favorite sweatshirt, and exchanging it for a brand-new shirt that you still have to break in.

As we are helping students to put on this new life, to bring together their faith and their everyday life, we need to realize that it won't be easy. Their competence in living the Christian life is strictly at a very conscious level. That is why, at first, they may feel that the demands of the Gospel are legalistic. They are concentrating so hard on staying within the boundaries, that it is hard for them to look to the goal, Jesus Christ.

If we are aware of this dynamic, we can remember a few important points that may help us to help them. Remember that the greatest immobilizer of young Christians is discouragement. They are thoroughly convinced that salvation is REALLY by works, and not by grace, and that if they make one more mistake, God will give up on them. They become like the little boy who kept going into his backyard and pulling up the plant to see if it had any roots yet. That kind of discouragement and self-doubt often leads to self-fulfilling prophecy.

Continue to emphasize the love and forgiveness of God. Teach them to rebound from sin, not by shaming them into repeated trips to the altar to *really* give it all to Jesus this time, but by encouraging them to confess their sin and get up again to walk.

Remember that kids often take their cue from us about how God looks upon them. If we give up on them, they will transfer that same sense of rejection to God.

Remind them that the Christian life is impossible; nobody can live it except Jesus. But now, Jesus is alive in them, and "it is God who works in you to will and to act according to his good purpose" (Philippians 2:13).

At this stage of the game, when they are still trying to stretch and strain to fit in the new clothes of life in Christ, I like to remind students of what Paul said in Philippians 1:4–6:

> In all my prayers for all of you, I always pray with joy because of your partnership in the gospel from the first day until now, being confident of this, that he who began a good work in you will carry it on to completion until the day of Christ Jesus.

Level Four: Unconscious Competence

I had the opportunity recently to visit with one of the students from my earliest years in youth ministry. Heather is now married, and she and her husband are overseeing a youth ministry of their own. She shared with me how God has shaped her life over the last fifteen years: "It hasn't always been smooth. But when I look at my life now, I can clearly see that some of the issues over which I once wrestled with God, I have now decisively placed under his hand."

What was even more exciting to see, was that now it seemed so natural for her to look at life from her new perspective under Christ, that it seemed as if she couldn't remember or imagine how she could have once felt differently under the old regime of self-rule. She wasn't for a moment saying that there aren't new areas that arise, and even minor skirmishes over some of the old turf. But some of the areas of her Christian walk that used to seem so strange to her now appear to be second nature.

As I listened, I was reminded of Paul when he wrote in Galatians 2:20, "I have been crucified with Christ and I no longer live, but Christ lives in me. The life I live in the body, I live by faith in the Son of God, who loved me and gave himself for me."

In Maslow's terminology, Heather has moved into the fourth level of learning, a stage of Unconscious Competence. She has begun to integrate her faith and her daily life to the point that it's almost as if she does it without thinking. Like the old Indian craftsman who has been weaving the rugs for so long that he doesn't even look at the needle any longer, Heather is at a point in her faith where she is unconsciously competent. She doesn't have to check and re-check herself, test and re-test her motives, surrender and re-surrender every decision; Christ is alive and living through her. This is the fullest expression of a faith that is lived out in everyday life.

This is no excuse for independence or arrogance (See Philippians 3:3–9.) To be sure, the Christian in this stage is not perfect, but at this point the course is set. Now it is a matter of finishing the race, living out what you know. As Paul put it:

> Not that I have already obtained all this, or have already been made perfect, but I press on to take hold of that for which Christ took hold of me. Brothers, I do not consider myself yet to have taken hold of it. But one thing I do: forgetting what is behind and straining toward what is ahead, I press on toward the goal to win the prize for which God has called me heavenward in Christ Jesus.
>
> All of us who are mature should take such a view of things. And, if on some point you think differently, that too God will make clear to you. Only let us live up to what we have already attained. (Philippian 3:12–16).

This is our goal as we nurture students: a faith that affects their everyday lifestyle. We may not see this during the junior or senior high-school years—but it is a goal to aim for. Students who are at the level of unconscious competence in living out the faith are students who have turned to the right channel. It is our responsibility to help them move forward by assisting them in the on-going process of fine tuning.

CHAPTER TEN
MAKING FAITH STICK

When we have some sense of how teenagers begin to work out their faith in everyday life, we can then start to strategize ways of nurturing a genuine lived-out faith in our youth groups.

1. *Post-Retreat Resolution.* Mike Yaconelli and his wife Karla, in their work with a Young Life club in their hometown of Yreka, California, have developed a good tool for helping students incorporate insights gained from a retreat into the fabric of their normal daily schedule once they return home. At the close of a weekend retreat or camp, Mike and Karla distribute to the students a list of possible resolutions they can make to begin to integrate their faith decisions with their daily lifestyle.

This can be a part of the closing worship service or it can be a part of a quiet time of meditation on the last day of camp. The list below gives examples of ideas for Post-Retreat Resolutions.

POST-RETREAT RESOLUTIONS

1. Write your parents a letter of affirmation.
2. Clean up your room for a week without being asked.
3. Give your parents a night off.
4. Clean the entire house while your parents are gone.
5. Clean the garage.
6. Wash your parents' car inside and out.
7. Mow the lawn.
8. Stack firewood.
9. Take care of your brothers/sisters for a night/weekend and give your parents a vacation.
10. Write your folks a long letter telling them what happened this week/weekend on our retreat.

11. Fix your parents breakfast in bed.
12. Fix dinner for the whole family.
13. Set aside a night when you can visit with your parents uninterrupted.
14. Tell your parents that instead of presents for your birthday, you would like money donated to Mexico/Haiti/etc. relief work.
15. Stay home for entire weekend just to be with family (no phone calls, no TV, no radio). Ground yourself.
16. Plan a family picnic.
17. Have a game night with your parents.
18. Clean up the kitchen and do dishes for a week.
19. Do family laundry for a week.
20. Set aside an hour per night for walking, jogging, tennis, etc. as a family.
21. Play no music (walkman, stereo, radio) for one week.
22. Stay off the phone for one week.
23. Plan a romantic night for your parents.
24. Tell (write) your steparent(s) how neat they are.
25. Put signs up welcoming your parents home.
26. Surprise parents by getting a group of friends and putting on a dinner for parents.
27. Give parents a coupon book (containing many of the things on this list or think up some of your own).
28. Improve your grades one point.
29. The next three times your parents say no to something you want to do, don't argue or pout, just say, "Oh, okay," and nothing else.

2. *Practical Bible Studies.* While it is certainly important that our students gain knowledge about various doctrinal truths, and while we will want to do various studies that survey particular biblical books, we should also spend an ample amount of time in topical Bible studies that explore teenagers' felt needs. These studies may utilize one particular biblical text, or several passages, or even be based on the biographical study of a particular biblical character. But they need to be focused on specific how-to topics. The list of topics below suggests some areas youth workers might want to explore with their group:

- How to use your mouth: Does God care how I talk?
- Living with my family: How to prevent parental runaway
- Dealing with temptation: Can the devil make you do it?
- Friendships that work
- How to correct a broken relationship
- To cheat or not to cheat: This is only a test
- Peer pressure: How to press on when your friends press in
- How to handle money: The question you hope to face
- What to do when someone is mad at you
- Honesty: Is it God's policy even when it isn't best?
- Music: Can I listen to rock and keep my name on the roll?
- Christian response to the media: "Be careful little eyes . . . "
- Masturbation: A scriptural look at the great unmentionable
- Making wise choices: Beyond eenie, meenie, miney, mo
- LUST: Thinking about the L word
- Sharing the faith without coming across as a jerk
- Self-image: Looking at myself from God's point of view
- Cliques, groups, and racism: "A swastika by any other name . . . "
- Survival skills for high school
- Prayer: An eye-opening experience
- How to understand the Bible
- Citizenship: What do I render unto Caesar?

Obviously, this list could be endless, but this will get you started thinking about areas in which teenagers will find the rubber of their Christian life meeting the road of their everyday experience. It probably is unwise to give students a diet of teaching solely based on these kinds of lifestyle themes. On the other hand, taking the time to discuss some of these practical issues helps our teens anchor their faith into their daily life at home or school or among friends.

3. *Short-term series.* One helpful off-shoot of the preceding idea is to make frequent use of Sunday school electives to examine specific topics in a short-term series. A three-to four-week study based on a specific area of interest will not only give your students added insight into that issue, but it may also spark additional interest in Sunday school.

It is also a fairly effective way of bringing in volunteer teachers who will commit only to a short-term assignment. That gives regular volunteers some time away, and it exposes new adult leadership prospects to the youth and the youth program.

4. *Develop a survey that will allow your students to evaluate their own effectiveness in living out the Christian life.* I put together the following survey several years ago to get my youth-group kids thinking and talking about their Christian life—areas of weakness, areas of strength, etc. The tool may be used in its present form or adapted to fit the needs of a specific program.

A SPIRITUAL CHECK-UP

Nobody likes going to the doctor. To begin with, sometimes you are asked to do things that make you feel a little uncomfortable: "Take off your clothes." "Fill up this bottle." "Bend over and cough."

On the other hand, it's not much fun to be sick, either. And an occasional check-up or physical performed by a good doctor can help us to keep our bodies in shape. Knowing this doesn't make the visit any more fun, but it does convince you of its value.

You're getting ready to take a test that will provide a check-up of your spiritual life. We promise you can keep your clothes on, you won't have to bend over, and you won't have to fill any funny bottles. But it still may be a little uncomfortable. You may feel the pressure of some probing questions, or you may feel the pain of some areas that you don't like thinking about.

Your honesty is important in this examination. Nobody is going to see your answers but you and the person giving you this test.

Some Suggestions:
1. Set aside at least forty-five minutes of quiet time to think through and write down your answers.
2. Keep your answers between you and God, to be shared only with the one person giving you this test.
3. Let's get together in about a week to go over the results of your examination.

4. Jesus is the Great Physician. Try to keep an open mind about how he might want to use this check-up in your own life.

I. *Pulse*: Are you a Christian?

A. Describe your relationship with Jesus Christ.

B. On a scale of 1 to 10 (1 = potential axe murderer, 10 = the next Mother Theresa), how would you rate your relationship with Christ? Why?

II. *Red Blood Cells* (carry the oxygen that prevents anemia and sluggishness).

A. Describe your devotional life.

1. Do you spend any time during the week reading the Bible or praying on your own? Describe these times and about how often you do this.

2. How would you like to see these times get better? And what do you think is keeping these devotions/quiet times from being all they could be?

B. Develop relationships that keep the arteries open.

1. In what ways do you feel that you and God have a friendship together?

2. Do you have a church fellowship where you try to regularly take part in Sunday worship? Describe.

III. *White Blood Cells* (disease fighters for inner cleansing and renewal).

A. How does your faith in Christ affect your ability to be accepting, loving, and forgiving?

B. How do you deal with feelings of guilt?

IV. *Brain Scan*: Check out your mind.

A. What are three of the biggest doubts or questions that you seem to struggle with?

B. What can you or are you doing to deal with those doubts and questions?

C. How would you describe your understanding of the Bible? Pick one of the following phrases that best sums up your ability to find helpful answers in the Bible. (a) Bible? What's a Bible? (b) I can't ever find anything I need when I need it; (c) I'm okay with the New Testament, but the Old Testament is like an old B movie with blurred subtitles; (d) I think I'm beginning to get more out of the Bible when other people teach or speak from it; (e) I'm a regular Bible whiz kid—next stop is memorization of Leviticus.

Explain your answer below.

D. How well do you feel you understand the basics of the Gospel? Try to write simple answers to the following questions:

1. What is sin?
2. What are the effects of sin?
3. Who is Jesus?
4. How does he deal with our sin?
5. Why does God offer us the gift of life with him?
6. How do you receive that gift?
7. Who is the Holy Spirit and where does he fit in all of this?
8. If you were a contestant on the TV game show, *Serious Pursuit*, and Vanna asked you to explain the following terms, which could you *not* explain? Circle them.

SANCTIFICATION   JUSTIFICATION   GRACE   FAITH CONFESSION   REPENTANCE   FRUIT OF THE SPIRIT

E. How would you describe your ability to fight off temptation? Choose the phrase below that best describes your approach. (1) Hot dog. This looks like fun! (2) Honk if you love Jesus. (3) Get the heck out of Dodge. (4) Pray. (5) Get with some people who are stronger than me. (6) Other.

F. How would you describe your self-image?

V. *Say ahhhhh*: A look at the tongue.

A. Would people who know you say that you spend more time encouraging people, competing with other people, or just ignoring other people?

B. What are some of the ways you build people up by what you say?

C. What are the situations in which you are most tempted to sin by telling a lie?

D. What types of situations trigger in you the temptation to cut someone down, either in jest or in anger?

E. Would your friends consider you a person who enjoys giving or receiving gossip?

VI. *Probing the Heart*.

A. Describe ways that you are trying to become more Christ-like in your thoughts and motives.

B. What priorities in your life bring you closer to God?

C. What priorities in your life might move you further away from God?

D. How are your relationships with friends affected by your commitment to Christ?

E. How are your relationships with your family affected by your commitment to Christ?

F. How are relationships with the opposite sex affected by your commitment to Christ?

VII. *Reflex Check*.

A. How are you responding to the people around you who rub you the wrong way?

B. How do you respond to the needs around you?

In your family?

Among your friends?

In other parts of the world?

C. How do you respond to failure?

D. How do you respond to success?

E. How do you respond to pressure (at home, school, work)?

VIII. *Eyes.*

A. What kind of vision do you have for how God might use you in the future?

B. What are some of the blind spots in your life that seem to keep getting you in trouble?

C. What guidelines do you use in trying to think about the movies and TV shows that are healthy for you to watch?

IX. *Hands.*

A. In what ways are you involved in meeting the needs of others?

B. What pressures keep you from working against injustices and other wrongs that you see around you?

C. How willing are you to turn your financial decisions over to God? How well is your Christian commitment expressed in your giving to the church or to those in need?

X. *Hearing.*

A. At what times do you feel like you can really hear God speaking to you?

B. What things keep you from hearing God's will better in your life?

C. What other voices and sounds (music) in your life might be drowning out what God wants you to hear?

X. *Feet.*

A. If the Christian life is more of a marathon than a sprint, how would you describe your ability to go for the long haul?

B. What weights keep you from running full speed ahead for God? What is holding you back or tempting you to go off-course?

C. Compared with where you were in your spiritual life one year ago, how would you describe where you are now?

THE BOTTOM LINE

When it is all said and done, there are two points we need to underline if our desire is to nurture a faith in our youth which will affect their daily lives. The first is something that needs to be said. The second is something that needs to be done.

It should be said that living out the Christian faith is never easy. Even when we walk by faith there will be those times when we stumble. Those of us who are involved in the ministry of Christian nurture must remember that discouragement and disillusionment are the two major factors that lead teenage Christians to walk out on their faith. They simply don't believe they can pull it off.

A teenage guy met with his youth minister for counsel about a very serious problem. He had come to talk with his youth minister because he could not overcome lust. He was angry. He was discouraged. He was mad. In a fit of frustration, he finally blurted, "Well, if God gave me these desires, why won't he let me satisfy them? I've had it. I'm going to pray right now—God, take away my sexual desire!" At which point the youth worker interrupted with, "Wait—I'm leaving the room in case he misses!"

A sense of defeat often convinces teenage Christians that they just can't cut it. They're not making the grade in school; they're not making the grade with the opposite sex; they're not making the grade in athletics; and now, they're not making the grade with God. Let's remember that one of our major responsibilities in helping students apply the word to their lives is to give large doses of encouragement, tempered and shaped by the grace of God.

But the number one way that we teach our youth about how to work out the faith in everyday life is by our own day-by-day modeling. We teach loudest by what we say, not by what we do. Paul wrote in 2 Timothy 3:10, 11, "You, however, know all about my teaching, my way of life, my purpose, faith, patience, love, endurance, persecutions, sufferings."

Paul's teaching curriculum was everyday life. If Timothy wanted to know how Paul's teaching could be applied to everyday life, he had only to watch Paul. That may be the greatest challenge and strategy of all, to help our students integrate their faith and everyday life by watching us do it. Our relationship with our spouse teaches volumes about the beauty of wholesome male/female relationships. Our use of our own time, money, skills, and resources gives a far more memorable lesson about these areas of life than any Bible study.

That means that one of the keys to helping students have that kind of discipleship that exists between the meetings, the kind of talk that walks, is to live out that kind of faith ourselves. In the words of Paul, "My message and my preaching were not with wise and persuasive words, but with a *demonstration* of the Spirit's power" (1 Corinthians 2:4).

CHAPTER ELEVEN
A DURABLE FAITH

Something happened when John moved into his high-school years. He never had been a candidate for Most Like Mother Theresa, but he was open and willing to listen. At the very least, he was compliant. His weekly attendance in junior high Bible study was consistent, if not zealous. For a junior higher, he seemed to be fairly normal!

Then came the divorce, a job change for his father, and a fairly significant decrease in his family's standard of living. Somewhere in the midst of John's fifteenth year of life, he left behind a family, a lifestyle, his junior high school, and (seemingly) his faith in God. When we began our fall youth-ministry program, John was noticeably AWOL.

I've met other Johns through my years of youth ministry—kids who seemed to be moving, slowly but surely, in the right direction (or who were, at least, stagnant facing the right direction!), and then some family crisis erupted, some relationship was ruptured, or something occurred that apparently shipwrecked a young faith in God. Sometimes there were no evident crises at all—just massive changes in a short period of time, to the point that a student who was showing signs of a budding Christian faith just seemed to have died on the vine.

To be sure, we never know how these stories will end. We only know that these stories usually have additional chapters. And we know that God has the capacity to raise the dead.

But that mustn't keep us from considering the fact that a faith characterized by footprints, rather than monuments (chapter 2), is a long-term faith, an enduring faith. We need to recognize that genuine discipleship is marked by a durable faith.

STORMS THAT
ROCK THE BOAT

When I think of John, or almost any of the hundreds of junior highers I've had a chance to spend time with through the years of my ministry, I am reminded of Peter. Good ol' Peter—always ready to make a commitment, even if he didn't know to what he was committing himself. Peter—the disciple with what seems a terminal case of hoof-and-mouth. Peter was the disciple who seems to me to be most like the modern youth groupee: excited, gung ho, quick to speak, exuberant, sometimes a study in obedience, sometimes a study in flakiness.

It was Simon Peter who witnessed, "You are the Christ, the Son of the Living God" (Matthew 16:16). But Peter's faith was somewhat cold-blooded and highly susceptible to changes in the environment. When Jesus announced his imminent betrayal on that Last Supper evening, Peter was the first one to speak up and pledge his willingness to die for Jesus (Matthew 26:31–33). And for approximately three to five hours, it would appear that he did hang tough. But as the environment changed, his commitment cooled. That sounds like an adolescent faith, doesn't it?

Peter was the one who couldn't wait to get out of the boat and walk on the water. This was going to be neat! Jesus was beckoning him to keep moving forward, deeper, closer. "Come," he said. Then Peter got down out of the boat, walked on the water, and came toward Jesus.

That's when he must have felt that gust of wind, that shift in wind direction, because that's when he panicked. Peter the Rock started to sink like a stone. "And beginning to sink, [he] cried out, 'Lord, save me!' Immediately Jesus reached out his hand and caught him. 'You of little faith,' he said, 'why did you doubt?' " (Matthew 14:25–31).

Can't you just see a Peter in your youth group . . . the kid who is always there, always gung ho, lovable, flaky, sometimes hot and sometimes cold? (No, I'm not describing some of your volunteer leaders.) All of the right confessions and commitments, and then, in the midst of a storm—panic, doubt, and sinking fast. The task of nurture mandates that we seek to stabilize that walk—that we nurture in students a durable faith.

FORECASTING THE STORMS

Most of us can well understand that sinking feeling. If we've been working long with teenagers, we've seen it before. We've even seen it in our own lives from time to time. But to make certain that we don't misunderstand the situation we need to be clear on one fact: doubt is neither the absence of faith nor the opposite of faith. When our teenagers go through storms of doubt and periods of turbulence, they have not necessarily forsaken their faith. Their faith may be wavering; it may be shaky; they may be sinking, but that is not the opposite of faith. It may mean the weakening of faith or that there is only a little faith (Matthew 14:31), but it does not mean *no* faith. Despite his doubts, Peter cried out, "*Lord*, save me" (Matthew 14:30).

Sometimes in youth ministry we undercut the student who is struggling and sinking because we jump to the conclusion that doubt is the absence of faith. That is not true. Doubt says, "*Unless* I see the nail marks in his hands . . . I will not believe it" (John 20:25). Non-faith says, "*Even if* I see the nail marks in his hands, I won't believe it." Without faith, it is impossible to be a Christian and to please God (Hebrews 11:6). But it is possible to be a Christian and doubt.

Doubt is a predictable part of adolescence. John's apparent sinking as he moved into high school was not an immediate trauma. There is something about moving into that part of life that causes storm clouds in most teenagers. We've discussed in earlier chapters some of the changes in cognitive development that accompany the physical changes. As students begin to think abstractly, and as life becomes less safe and protected, episodes of struggle and doubt will occur. These questions are intensified by difficult events like the break-up of family, the loss of a friend, or the emergence of faith questions that aren't so easily answered as they were in Vacation Bible School.

When children are young, they think in a concrete terms. It is a fairly simple matter to get them to sing, "Jesus loves me, this I know, for the Bible tells me so." But as that child begins to move into the early teen years, new questions emerge. We shelter our children from some of these questions during their younger years, and rightly so. But these shelters no longer hold up to the storms of adolescence.

A fifteen-year-old wonders, "If Jesus loves me, how come he allowed my parents to divorce?" A fourteen-year-old begins to feel the pressure of non-believing friends and begins to question her own faith and her own beliefs. A thirteen-year-old stands in front of the mirror and asks the reflection, "If God loves me so much, why does my body looks like this? Why am I so dumb in school? Why does my complexion look like a pizza?" And all of a sudden, the childhood confessions are questioned and rewritten: "Jesus loves me, this I think; but why is this zit as big as the sink?"

That doesn't for a moment mean that the old answers are necessarily wrong. If we start messing around with those, as some have begun to do, we will be making a big mistake. The Word of God, with all of its old answers, is just as true. The problem is that now there are new questions. And somehow, the old answers sometimes don't seem to fit anymore.

NEW QUESTIONS

A host of new questions bombard teenagers, and the old answers of earlier years are unsatisfactory. While there are probably as many different questions and doubts as there are teenagers, there are certain categories of questions that seem to be fairly common among adolescents.

1. *"Why do I keep messing up everything?"* The generic term for this brand of question is *discouragement*. Teenagers have been moving through their childhood years with the spoken and unspoken assumption that when they grow up, things will be better. They will hit that growth spurt that their parents keep telling them about. They will eventually get the hang of algebra and their grades will turn around. They will make that once-and-for-all commitment to Christ that will usher them into a new era of right decisions and unclouded motivations.

But of course, most of the time, life doesn't happen that way. The sixteen-year-old young man is coming to grips with the fact that there isn't going to be some cataclysmic growth spurt. This is it. The hoped for career as the next All-Universe basketball star probably will not materialize. Or, a seventeen-year-old girl finally realizes that her breasts are never going to produce ample cleavage. Whatever blossoming is supposed to happen, has happened. The growing season is almost over.

While these situations may make an adult reader smile, they can be extremely discouraging to a teenager wondering, "Why me?" or more likely, "Why not me?"

The teenage years are filled with supposed conclusions, premature though they may be: the sophomore who comes to the conclusion that he just isn't going to strike it big academically; the junior girl who begins to think that maybe she just isn't attractive to guys—that the Prince Charming she dreamed about as a little girl is not going to come, and she may not even be invited to her junior prom; or the senior who finally admits that any hopes of getting a scholarship for college or being accepted into a pre-med program are simply unrealistic optimism.

Ken's parents were upper-middle class people who deeply loved their children. The last thing they wanted was to cause their children hurt and disillusionment. That's why I was so surprised that they had forced Ken to take the SAT nineteen times until he came up with a score with which they were satisfied. Ken told me that what he had learned from the test, from his special tutor, and from the whole process, was that somehow he just didn't have it. "What's wrong with me?" he wondered.

Katie, an attractive and likeable teenage girl, sat in my office. Her warm smile and kind attitude had made her one of those youth-group kids it was easy to love. I found it hard to believe that behind her smile were the wounds of a broken relationship. She had really cared for this guy, and it had all seemed so wonderful. But now he had asked her if they could just be friends. We talked together and we prayed together. I told her all the right things, reminded her of all the right promises. And yet I could hear her eyes responding, "Yes, but those promises don't seem to apply to me."

One of the major immobilizers of teenage Christians is the sense that they simply do not measure up, physically, academically, intellectually, or spiritually. They just aren't getting on par. They are getting older, and they *aren't* getting better. And bending low under the weight of unreasonable, or at least, unfulfilled expectations, the discouraged adolescent begins to ask questions that are not easily answered.

2. *"But that's not right . . . "* It's called *apparent contradictions*.

A student approaches you and says, "You've always told us that if we are Christians, we should date only other Christians. Well, I have dated five of the guys in this youth group, and every one of them was all hands. And the only guy who treats me like a lady is the guy who sits next to me in English, and he says he's an atheist. Now, whom should I date?"

Or how about this one: One of your strongest Christian kids comes to you, obviously disappointed and confused. "I don't understand it," he confesses. "You tell us in Bible study that the Bible says, 'The way of the transgressor is hard.' Well, I just 'righteousness-ed' my way to a D on the calculus exam, and the kid that sits next to me just 'transgressed' his way to a B+. Next week, when I miss the ski retreat because I'm on restriction for a low grade in calculus, I'll try to remember who had it 'hard.' "

Or another sticky situation: One of the younger girls in your youth group approaches you with complete sincerity to say, "Look, I know you've told us that homosexuality is wrong and that homosexuals, drunkards, and fornicators will not inherit the kingdom of God and all that. But you know, the only adult in our entire school who treats us like human beings is the volleyball coach, and she says she's a lesbian. And the two faculty members who are always talking to us about Jesus treat everybody like jerks. I don't understand what is so bad and sinful about Ms. Watkins."

Those are tough questions. But they're real questions—the kind of questions that test our teenagers' faith everyday. They come as a result of situations that seem to say, "This is what you were taught—but this is the way it is." Sure, there are explanations, and there are ways of dealing with these questions. But when you are a Christian in the ninth grade, they appear to be contradictions of facts you thought you knew you could count on.

Mr. Spainer was the teacher in charge of the debate team at the high school. From all I could tell, he must have had a winsome personality—one of those teachers at the high school who makes just enough "off-the-cuff" comments about the administration or the educational system to be considered radical by the students. They admired his unorthodox teaching methods. They admired the fact that he made them think.

Unfortunately, Mr. Spainer's favorite sport was making fun of the Christian faith. Even more unfortunate was the fact that several of my key leadership students were members of the debate team. And this was an active debate team—tournaments almost every weekend, team retreats, total involvement. His influence in these students' lives was very real, and he had the added advantage of being around these students in the hallways and lunchroom at school.

A few weeks seldom went by without students coming to report some new comment or insight shared by Mr. Spainer. It was obvious that he was raising some questions that were troubling these students. Since they couldn't answers his questions, they wondered if there were answers at all. There were, of course, plausible and reasonable answers. But for a high-school student who has tremendous respect for his teacher, the words of that teacher are accepted as nearly infallible.

If we are committed to nurturing a durable faith in the lives of our students, we will need to prepare them for these very real and difficult questions. They were not unfair questions. They may have been investigated unfairly, but the questions themselves were legitimate. Building in students a durable faith means working through the questions with them, perhaps even asking them ourselves in the context of the youth group.

When this has been suggested in youth worker workshops, some have protested, "But aren't you planting the seeds of doubt in these kids' minds by asking tough questions?" I don't think so. The bottom line, as we observed in the preceding paragraphs, is that life itself causes doubt. Life raises questions. We are simply choosing the arena within which our students will deal with their doubts.

3. *"I'm just not sure what I want to do."* I call this one, *the reality of responsibility*. There is a certain freedom in being given no choices. Part of the freedom of childhood is the absence of difficult decisions

concerning day-to-day living. Someone else makes those choices for children. The majority of children are free to play and go to school and have fun, with the assurance that there is someone controlling enough of their environment that they can't endanger themselves too much by wrong decisions. In a sense, their freedom grows out of parental restriction.

But most of that kind of freedom ends during adolescence. It is exchanged for the more authentic and risky freedom of being able to choose one's own restrictions and boundaries. During the teenage years we transfer the choices to the youth, and it is now up to them, in the words of one comedian, "to mess up their own lives without parental interference."

To begin with, at approximately sixteen years of age, a teenager is granted a driver's license. This in itself, has remarkable ramifications. Try to remember the first time you sat down behind the wheel of a car with your driver's license and there was no one else in that car. Mom or Dad were not sitting over there in the passenger seat monitoring velocity, direction, and passenger activity. It was quite a moment.

I remember the intoxicating freedom of that first morning, driving myself to school, and realizing that if I wanted to keep driving, there was nothing stopping me from driving to California, or Myrtle Beach, South Carolina, or even New York City. It was an incredible feeling. As I stepped out of the car in the school parking lot, I relished the idea that today for the first time, I had come here of my own accord (although I was not actually driving a Honda at the time).

But the intoxication of freedom also brought with it some sobering realities. Where I went and with whom I went was now clearly up to me. This car gave me a lot of opportunities for sin and wrong-doing. For the first time, I was forced to make my own choices and to find out what I would choose to do when given the freedom to decide. All of those years growing up I had said, "I would never do this or that because it's wrong." And now that I actually could, I was about to discover whether I would do those things or not.

As students move into high school, they are also forced to think more and more seriously about their future. "Where am I headed? What will I do with my life?" For the first time, these teenagers can see a glimmer of light at the end of the academic tunnel. They are realizing that they will not be in school forever—which again, means authentic freedom to spend one's days as one wishes, but with the risk that one's bad choices may have costly consequences.

That freedom brings with it a whole new category of questions. "Do I really believe what I say I believe? And if I do believe it, am I willing to live out those beliefs? What will I do when I encounter friends whose beliefs are quite different from mine? Now that parental limitations are being lifted, what self-imposed limitations, if any, will there be? I think I know who I am, but if I am really that person, then I wouldn't be making these choices, I wouldn't be involved in these kinds of activities. Which makes me wonder: Am I who I've always thought I was?"

These questions are neither unhealthy nor unnatural. They are a part of maturing into adulthood. They come along with the territory of developing a healthy autonomy. But they can still be frightening questions. And these kinds of questions can put students in a spiritual headlock, which can eventually pin them down if they lack a durable faith.

IS THERE FAITH
AFTER HIGH SCHOOL?

As a youth minister-turned-college professor I can't help but notice them every autumn as I walk across our campus. I can't help but think about the fact that these new fresh-faced freshmen wandering our campus, trying desperately to attract attention and yet remain anonymous, are people who only a few weeks ago were members of somebody's youth group.

I've noticed their mixed emotions. I've heard their unspoken resolutions, their undeclared plans, and their unconfessed doubts, and my guess is that we both suspect that their adventure in these next four years will leave a life-long impression. Perhaps it is because I think like a youth minister, or because I live among them as a teacher, that I have come to believe that one of the greatest tests of the durability of our students' commitments comes after high school when they graduate from youth group and go away to college.

The real tests that they face over those next few years will have little to do with modern civilization and organic chemistry. They will face tough questions for which they have been given no texts, and one of their greatest resources during this time of examination and discovery will be the training and preparation that they received before they ever set foot on our campus. (Portions of this section originally appeared in a resource for youth groups entitled *Hot Topics*, David C. Cook Publishing, used by permission.)

WELCOME TO
WHAT ABOUT U.

What questions and issues will they be wrestling with? Some will be similar to the questions they confronted in high school, such as the questions mentioned in the preceding paragraphs. And yet, in the college years, the questions seem to take on even more weight and urgency. Here is a sampling of the curriculum:

• **Identity 202.** Away from the old friends and family members who might never let them get away with a drastic change of lifestyle or life direction, one of the key questions for these incoming freshmen will be the question of identity: *Who will I be?*

Obviously, exploring one's own identity begins as early as childhood. But it is during the high-school and college years that one must make a commitment to an identity. There are decisions to be made, vocations to be chosen, and goals to be set, and the college years bring with them an ominous sense that, beginning now, the choices count—from here on out, we keep score.

• **Religion 101.** *What do I really believe?* As we have seen in earlier chapters, one of the characteristics of adolescent spirituality is that it is heavily influenced by relationships. The college years force young people to confront the issue of whether this Christian faith is really their own.

They find themselves in a college dorm with people whose god is very different from the god of the youth group, the god of mom or dad, or the God of scripture. That's when they really begin to find out whether they actually believe what they think they believe.

- **Ethics 101.** Closely linked to the first two courses is this third one in which the curriculum deals with moral choices — *choices relating to sexuality, personal habits, issues of integrity*. Many students graduate into the college years appearing to be people of firm moral conviction. But after the first few weekends of the semester, it is quickly evident who actually has moral convictions and who has previously lived a moral life due to the lack of opportunity for immorality.

It is one thing to decide not to have sex with your girlfriend when you don't have many opportunities to be alone anyway. But when you are living in an open dorm with unlimited visiting hours and your roommate offers to stay lost until tomorrow, the only thing between you and immorality is genuine moral conviction.

Quite frankly, too many college students have never been prepared for that kind of freedom. Their choices have been based on the rules of someone else, or the lack of genuine opportunity. Moral values based on that kind of foundation often resemble the house built upon the sand. When the temptation comes, so does moral collapse.

- **Economics 101.** Another area that college students must begin to explore surrounds the combined issues of *career choice and financial goals*. More than any other single issue, this seems to be the one that actually preoccupies college students.

Whereas some research shows that freshmen entering college fifteen years ago listed "the development of a meaningful philosophy of life" as a major goal for their college experience, more recent research shows that this was a goal for only twenty percent of the freshman class of 1988. The number one issue was finding a financially-rewarding career.

- **Theology 100.** (pre-requisite: Religion 101) This is a course that will be particularly important for students who enter college with a firm commitment to the faith. The main agenda here will be: *Why do I believe what I believe?* Religion professors seem to consider fall of the freshman year the open season for shooting down young Christians in their faith. Sometimes of course, their intent is to help students reinforce their personal beliefs in Scripture. Other times, their intent is far less positive.

By the time the semester ends, the classroom will be littered with the scalps of some frail Christians whose faith was overpowered and intimidated into a back corner of their mind by some professor whose intellectual credentials proved more convincing than the lessons and flannel graphs of the Sunday school back home.

• **Family Life 300.** Oh, yes—there is the matter of meeting a mate in college! Most college students deny the old joke that they are going to college for an M.R.S. degree, but that doesn't override the fact that *an overwhelming number of college students will leave campus this spring not only with a diploma, but also with a spouse.* And long after one has agonized through the choice of a major, there will still be the consequences and effects of the choice of a mate.

Admittedly, this may not be a required course, but it is without question the most serious subject matter in the curriculum of college experience.

BUILDING STAYING POWER

So many times, we get near-sighted in youth ministry and begin thinking that our job is to help students survive high school. But our real goal is to equip students for the long haul—to help students develop a faith that survives and thrives apart from the umbilical cord of the youth group—even as they move into the college years and beyond.

Unfortunately, quick-fix strategies for forging a durable faith don't work. But we can help our students weather these storms of questions without sinking under the waves. The key is helping youth build a network of support relationships which will help them to understand that struggle is normal and that there are people who will support them and walk with them through the times of struggle without making them feel that they are about to lose their salvation.

STRUCTURING A NETWORK OF SUPPORT

One of the ways to nurture a support fellowship is to build some variation of the Covenant Group. We developed the Covenant Group program in our ministry to give students an arena in which they could share their burdens and victories with one another in an atmosphere of support and encouragement.

Each new school semester the students were sent a notice about the beginning of a new thirteen-week Covenant Group experience. Covenant Group was open to students in ninth grade or higher who were willing to agree to and abide by the terms of the Covenant. Essentially, that meant being at Covenant Group every Tuesday morning at 6:30, and bringing with them a journal entry they had written about their life with Jesus in the preceding week.

The commitment was limited to thirteen weeks because this seemed to make it less intimidating to students who wanted to try it out, but not commit themselves to a lifetime contract. Students who wanted to continue their commitment to Covenant Group could simply sign up for another thirteen weeks.

Membership was limited to ninth grade or older because it was a co-ed group that involved some pretty intense intimacy. It seemed unreasonable to expect seventh grade guys to make themselves vulnerable to that kind of intimacy. If one of the pre-ninth grade students wanted this kind of experience, and many did, they could take part in the Small Group program, in which groups of the same sex met weekly. In many ways, the two programs were similar, except that the Covenant Group involved a little more commitment.

Sitting week after week in Covenant Group, listening to kids read their journals to one another and share their lives, I experienced some of the most satisfying and moving moments in my youth ministry. Predictably, at first students were reluctant to open up. But after testing the water and finding the group was a safe place where their wounds, questions, and victories would be respected, their honesty was amazing.

Students would read their journals, one at a time, around the breakfast table, and then there would be a period of prayer. I remember Renee' telling us of the terrible arguments her parents were having, and of her fear that they might split up. I remember David talking about his concern that his father, now divorced and living away from home, was continuing to harass his mom. He wasn't sure how a Christian guy was supposed to handle that kind of thing. Often there were tears. Frequently there was laughter. These sessions contained no intentional Bible teaching, yet many truths were learned. And more often than not, breakfast would end with a warm hug and a piping hot cinnamon bun for the road.

Covenant Groups are founded on a simple idea: Let the students be the church to each other. Let them be the body of Christ and bear one another's burdens. No extensive preparation is required. No program was more often identified by our former students as the part of our ministry that most helped them in their Christian walk.

HOW TO HELP WITH
THE TOUGH QUESTIONS

1. *Skeptics Night Out.* Jackson Crum at Church of the Savior in Wayne, Pennsylvania, has a unique meeting periodically that is specifically designed to address some of the tough faith questions that students have to face. Students are encouraged to bring their non-Christian friends from school so there is an authenticity to these sessions.

Questions range from, "How do we know we can trust the Bible?" to "What about all of those big-name preachers who are messing around?" to "How come Christians say you're going to hell just because you don't believe they way they do?"

Students can submit questions anonymously, and they are addressed, one at a time, either by a panel of people or by one appointed person. This could be the youth minister, a pastor, or someone else who has a knowledge of the Christian faith, a knowledge of the ways teenagers think, and most important, the honesty to admit that they don't have all the answers. The idea is not to demonstrate that every question has an answer. The idea is to demonstrate that there is enough credibility to the Christian faith that we can decide to trust God even when we don't know the answers.

2. *Tension Getters/Case Studies. Tension Getters* (Youth Specialties/ Zondervan, 1985), edited by Mike Yaconelli and David Lynn, helps students work through some of the tough questions in the youth-group setting before they have to face them in the lunchroom or locker room, where there is considerably less support.

For example, here's a typical tension getter:

You are talking with a friend at school. Your friend has just started coming to youth group, which is a good thing, because now more than ever, he needs support. His father just died last week. He was a good man, the kind of father that any family would want to have: kind, gracious, caring, and lots of fun. However, he never seemed to have much time for God. He felt that it was "okay . . . just not for (him)." Now that the funeral is over and your friend is trying to get things back to normal, he asks you if his father is now in heaven. What is your response?

A tension getter or case study like this could be used in a group-setting in which you would ask groups of three or four students to wrestle with the issue and combine their thoughts to write up a response. Or a youth worker might choose to give students the assignment of role-playing this conversation. That would give the added input of not only the response, but the friend's reaction to the response. Or students can be encouraged to work out their own individual responses to the tension getter, and then share their responses with the group.

Along with utilizing *Tension Getters* (and its cousins, *Tension Getters 2*, *Amazing Tension Getters*, and *Option Play*), with a little creativity and thoughtfulness you can write your own tension getters. The home-grown case studies have the added advantage of allowing the youth worker to address specific issues being faced by his or her group.

The key is to create a situation that puts students in a quandary about what might be the proper response. Then, stand back and bite your lip. Students should understand clearly that there they will not be judged for their response, right or wrong, to the situation. Remember, the goal here is to maintain a safe arena for the open discussion of these issues.

3. *Train students in theology.* In chapter five we discussed the importance of nurturing in students a faith that affects the head as well as the heart. Part of that nurture will have to involve giving students some basic foundational theological training. It will need to be

learner-centered; it will need to initiate active learning techniques (see chapter five); and, it must be done.

To be sure, training in theology is not the sort of thing that causes a surge in adolescent adrenaline, but it can be conducted in such a way that students understand, for example, how our faith in the sovereignty of God does affect our everyday life. We are kidding ourselves if we think theology does not affect our students. Every teenager in your youth group has a theology, and that theology, however incomplete and primitive, has a tremendous influence on the way they look at the tough questions in their everyday lives.

In *Facing Turbulent Times* (Tyndale, 1981) Gordon McDowell recounts a Peanuts comic strip in which there is a discussion between Linus and Lucy. Looking out the window at flashes of lightning and the thunderous fury of a summer storm, Lucy comments, "What if it rains so hard that the whole world is flooded?" The ever-cool, ever-aware Linus responds with a stiff lip, "Not to worry. In Genesis, chapter 9, verses 13 and 14, God assured Noah that he would never again flood the entire earth, and the sign of the rainbow is a reminder of his promise."

"Whew," Lucy responds. "That sure makes me feel better."

Linus, glib as usual, answers, "Yes. Sound theology has a way of doing that." And so it does.

DICK AND JANE
GO TO COLLEGE

Thinking specifically of how we might better prepare our youth for their college experience, consider the following suggestions:

1. *We need to do more teaching about the Christian idea of vocation—that God has called all of us to ministry.* Because we have neglected this area of Christian teaching, we are graduating students who have no idea that God is interested in their careers. In short, they need to understand that the Wonderful Counselor wants also to be our career counselor. Some suggested passages for study: Colossians 3:23–25, 1 Peter 2:9–10, Romans 12:1–12.

2. *Introduce your students to various campus ministries.* A number of youth ministers are now taking their seniors on one-day field trips

to the colleges they will be attending so that they can put them in touch with some of the people on that campus doing ministry. Representatives from InterVarsity, Campus Crusade, or Navigators would probably welcome the opportunity to have lunch with you and one of your students to share what they are doing on campus.

3. *Acquaint your students with Christian literature.* I doubt that I would have survived the principalities and powers of my college religion courses if I had not been introduced to the writings of C.S. Lewis, J.I. Packer, R.C. Sproul, F.F. Bruce, John Stott, and others.

Being firmly convinced that a reading Christian is a growing Christian, I have always made it one of my goals in ministry to put in the hands of my high-school students good Christian books. Most high-school kids don't even know such books exist. It is our responsibility and opportunity to incite that interest.

4. *Guide your kids in a study of how to discern God's will* (see chapter twelve). Of special importance is helping students think through the difference between the precepts of God ("Thou shalt not commit adultery") and the principles of God ("Do not make your brother stumble").

They will need to understand that sometimes God's guidance will come to them as much through application of the principles as through application of the precepts—particularly when it comes to everyday gray areas and dilemmas of guidance they will face during the college years.

(5) Talk openly and honestly about the reality that many of them over the next four years will find a life-partner. My personal recommendation is that perhaps in separate small groups of guys and girls you work through Walter Trobisch's classic little book, *I Married You* (Harper & Row, 1975). It's an excellent primer for some of the important questions that surround this topic.

THE FINAL EXAM

Life has a way of testing our ministries, and testing our fruit, to see if they stand up under the scrutiny of everyday living. This is always a little discomforting, especially when those who are being tested are people in whom we have invested lots of love and hard work. As we consider ways to nurture a durable faith in the lives of our students we must be wise and creative in our use of the various ministry strategies mentioned above. But we should remember that our efforts are not alone. We work in tandem with a God who is committed to building a lasting faith in our youth. Even when those graduating seniors walk away from the youth group and leave our presence, they are not leaving God's. "He who began a good work in [them] will carry it on to completion until the day of Christ Jesus" (Philippians 1:6).

CHAPTER TWELVE
A FAITH BECOME FLESH

It was one of those beautiful golden afternoons in the White Mountains of New Hampshire. I was with my youth group on a backpacking trip, and we were perched atop a one-thousand-foot-high piece of granite called Bond Cliffs. We were there to enjoy the view, and to enjoy the experience of walking backwards down the first one hundred feet of Bond Cliffs in an exercise rock climbers call rappelling. Basically, it involves attaching oneself to a safety line, facing the cliff, stepping backwards, and descending along a length of rope in a controlled(!) fall.

Molly was the first of the girls in our group to go down. She was always ready for anything, a natural athlete, and to her, this looked like it could be exciting. Unfortunately, it was a bit more exciting than she had expected.

With her back to the drop, she leaned back to put tension in the safety line. For a safe rappel, it's important to lean backwards off the cliff so that there is enough tension in the rope that the climber's body is perpendicular to the face of the cliff. This first step back, leaning out over a one-thousand-foot drop, doesn't come naturally to most folks.

Always gung ho, Molly leaned back with characteristic gusto. That was good. Unfortunately, as she leaned back, she fell backwards with enough momentum that her feet slipped upwards off the face of the cliff. That was bad. Within the span of a blink, Molly found herself upside down, swinging back and forth one-thousand-feet above the floor of the valley . . . which was not what she had intended.

She screamed. Some of the other kids screamed. I think I screamed. Actually, she wasn't really at any risk. We hoisted her back up using the safety line and she was on solid ground again (right side up) inside of two minutes. But the adventure had grabbed everyone's attention.

That night, back around the campfire, after Molly had put on some dry pants, we took some time to discuss the episode. Several students shared various comments, and then Molly spoke up and made what I thought was an intriguing observation. "You know," she said, "all my life I've grown up in a Christian home, where we talk about faith in God and about trusting God. But today was the first time in my life I think I really discovered what it meant to trust God."

Me too, Molly.

LESSONS FROM A CLIFF-HANGER

Helping students to develop a real-life faith means helping students to flesh out their faith—not just to talk about the faith, or hear the testimonies of those who have lived out the faith—but to be put in a position that forces them to experience and explore their own faith in God.

Too many of our students move through their youth-group experience hearing earnest people describe the importance of faith, and how God can help us in our time of need, but they never have to test their own faith. They are seldom forced or encouraged to flesh out what they think they believe.

Like most of us, the average teenage Christian charts out a course through the week that allows for minimum risk, attempting only what, in all likelihood, they could pull off without God's help. So opportunities seldom arise to learn the adventure of walking by faith. It's only in those rare moments of cliff-hanging that we get to see that word *faith* become flesh. And in those episodes our faith is both affirmed and strengthened.

David Elkind, child psychologist at Tufts University, talks in his writing about the importance of giving kids markers, experiences that represent important steps forward in their lives. Although he writes in the context of secular development, citing experiences like getting a driver's license, a first kiss, a first job, or high-school graduation, his point is equally valid as we try to nurture spiritual development. Whether it is a concrete instance of giving a cup of cold water in Jesus' name by serving on a missions project, or genuinely trusting God to help them attempt something beyond their means, such as singing a solo in the youth musical, kids need spiritual markers they can look to as episodes in which they truly encountered God.

Garry Shirk, former youth minister of Christ United Methodist Church in Jackson, Mississippi, actually encouraged his youth group to build a marker in their youth room as a reminder of the particularly dramatic way God had worked on one of their recent retreats. The students were encouraged on the last day of the camp to go out and find a rock that would represent what God had shown them or taught them during the camp.

Then, after each student had painted his or her name on the rock, they all brought the stones back to the church. There, in the youth room, like the people of Israel in the Old Testament, they raised an Ebenezer (1 Samuel 7:12) to remind themselves of the way their faith had been experienced in a real and dramatic way on that trip.

MARKERS AGAINST YOU

One might reasonably ask why we would say in one chapter (chapter four) that real-life discipleship is marked by footprints and not by monuments, and then turn around in a subsequent chapter and seemingly suggest that kids need to have these monument experiences. Good question.

What is important here is that students need opportunities to flesh out their faith. They need these monument experiences. But the key is that we see these episodes as milestones and do not allow them to become tombstones. The students are not going to fall off a cliff every day. They are not going to see their faith fleshed out in dramatic ways every day or every week. It is wonderful when they do. But we need to be careful not to allow them to be constantly waiting for the next time or looking back to the last time.

I was talking with a youth minister recently whose main source of frustration was that his kids seem to keep looking back to the previous summer's camp as their source of joy and encouragement. And by his own account, it had been a wonderful time for his group. Several students had become Christians, and two or three had made dramatic breakthroughs in their spiritual walk. But of course, as last summer becomes more and more distant, their encouragement and joy diminishes. Now, he said, "It seems as if my kids keep wanting us to re-create last summer's camp experience, instead of looking ahead to what God wants to do among us now."

Many of our students live from summer camp to summer camp, choir tour to choir tour, retreat to retreat, and never realize that there is life between the monuments. Real-life discipleship is about the footprints that lead forth from these episodes. These experiences are milestones that help us make progress, and not tombstones where we drop dead.

LEARNING THROUGH EXPERIENCE

The irony of providing opportunities for students to flesh out their faith is that so often, it is through the unplanned events that we experience the need to trust God and put our faith to the test. We had not planned for Molly to do a back flip off of Bond Cliffs. We had planned to rappel. But in the course of the planned activity, the unplanned happened, and it was through the unplanned that a student discovered what it really means to trust God.

Hence, one of the difficulties of helping students to stretch their faith muscles is that every effort is taken to make sure an activity is safe—no real risks. Yet it's not until we attempt that which is risky that we learn to trust God to help us complete the task.

So often in our youth programs, we go out of our way to make sure kids are not put in uncomfortable situations. We don't ask them to lead this Bible study because standing up in front of their peers might scare them. We protect them from the consequences of bad decisions because we want to help them. We don't pressure them to try something new because it might make them feel awkward. But those kinds of circumstances are precisely what force them to reach beyond themselves and their own resources.

Paul's letter to Timothy seems to suggest this very same dynamic when he writes in 2 Timothy 3:10–11:

> You, however, know all about my teaching, my way of life, my purpose, faith, patience, love, endurance, persecutions, sufferings—what kinds of things happened to me in Antioch, Iconium, and Lystra, the persecutions I endured. Yet the Lord rescued me from all of them.

It's impossible to read this passage without noting that Timothy's greatest lessons about faith were not the ones he heard, but the ones he knew about and had observed, especially when circumstances were difficult. Paul recalls sufferings, and persecutions, and what happened to him at Antioch, Iconium, and Lystra. It doesn't sound as if Paul is recalling pleasant memories here. A quick look through the passage also reveals words such as *patience* and *steadfastness*, notions such as endurance and rescue. These are lessons learned only under difficult circumstances.

I spoke at Creation '89, a huge music festival held in the summertime in the farm country of central Pennsylvania's rolling hills. From day one the festival was plagued by horribly inclement weather: rain storms, extreme flooding, and mud that was inches deep. Several performances were interrupted by torrential downpours. Because of the flooding, drinking water had to be rationed, campers had to be towed out of the mud, and whole campsites just floated away, tents and all. In short, it was a mess.

But every teenager I spoke with at that festival, and many with whom I have spoken since then, have said that it was the best Creation they had been to in years. One youth leader told me that her group was more unified through the adverse conditions, and that her kids were less distracted than in years past because the weather had a way of making the group get focused on what the festival was all about.

A number of youth ministers have echoed these same sentiments, remarking to me that there was more spiritual growth in their group through that year's festival than in any year past. Why? Because what befell us in those three days of mud, flood, and crud forced us to look beyond ourselves, our own resources, and our own circumstances, and rediscover what it means to trust God.

PLANNING FOR THE UNPLANNED

The psychologist Carl Rogers talks about learning that only takes place only from the neck up. Unfortunately, much of what our students know about the Christian life has been learned in just those terms. And yet, we know that the best way to learn something is not by working it into our brain but by working it out in our lives, our everyday experiences. Someone has put it this way: "Tell me and I'll forget; show me and I'll remember; walk with me and I'll understand."

A wise youth minister will make full use of strategies, resources, and activities that emphasize experiential learning — learning through experience. The educator Edgar Dale utilized the following diagram to explain how we learn better through concrete experiences than through abstract teaching.

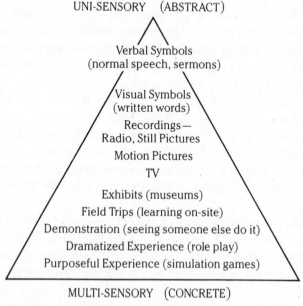

UNI-SENSORY (ABSTRACT)

Verbal Symbols
(normal speech, sermons)

Visual Symbols
(written words)

Recordings—
Radio, Still Pictures

Motion Pictures

TV

Exhibits (museums)

Field Trips (learning on-site)

Demonstration (seeing someone else do it)

Dramatized Experience (role play)

Purposeful Experience (simulation games)

MULTI-SENSORY (CONCRETE)

Cone of Experience, Audio-Visual Methods in Teaching, 1969, Holt, Rinehart & Winston

If we learn best through experience, then it makes sense that we learn best about faith through concrete experiences that flesh out.

Since few of us are willing to push our kids off a cliff, and since none of us have any control over thunderstorms and mud slides, we need to consider alternative ways to give our students opportunities to flesh out their faith. How can we put students in circumstances that force them to explore their own faith in God?

Actually, it may not be as difficult as it sounds. There are a number of activities that can take students out of their own comfort zone long enough to force them to fall back on their own faith. Some of these activities utilize stress or some form of deprivation that will bring a student to the boundaries of her own safety zone. Others are contrived experiences, simulation games, action parables, and role-playing activities—experiences which put students in a position of having to flesh out their faith. Let's look at both types of strategies.

ALL STRESSED UP AND NO PLACE TO GROW

One of the most successful programs worldwide for helping people from all walks of life to gain a good perspective is Outward Bound, a group that has gained an international reputation for providing controlled experiences in which people test and discover their own personal limits.

Outward Bound got its start in an interesting way. Back in World War II the British navy was finding that its youngest sailors were not able to survive the rigors of drifting for a few days in a lifeboat after having their ships torpedoed at sea. The older sailors, in the same situation, had a markedly better survival rate, for no apparent reason other than that their lifestyle had not been as sophisticated as that of the younger sailors who had grown up with more modern conveniences.

The decision was made to start a special program (later to be called Outward Bound) for the younger sailors in which they would be put in controlled situations of stress and deprivation. The results were remarkable. The young apprentice seamen who had been through the program learned to cope with stress much more effectively and had a significantly greater rate of survival in combat situations.

It isn't necessary to wait for a thunderstorm. We needn't camp in the middle of a mud pit. We needn't think of torpedoes as an essential youth-ministry resource. A wide range of activities can nurture within our students a faith that is concrete. Here are some suggestions:

1. *Mission Trips*

There may be no single activity that is more effective at helping students to flesh out their faith than getting them into a setting of service. This is especially the case if the setting is cross-cultural, where a teenager might have to reckon with the strange, undefined threat of an inner-city ghetto, or the inconceivable poverty of a Haitian back country village, or the unanswerable stare of a starving child who is wasting away in some third-world orphanage. These kinds of experiences extend us to the limit emotionally, physically, and spiritually.

Charlie was an upbeat guy, a star soccer player at the high school, a teenager who had grown up with the nurture of committed Christian parents. It was hard to teach him about faith, because everything seemed to be going so well in his world. Who needs faith when you're sixteen years old, a popular senior with lots of girlfriends, and you have parents who love you? It was almost too easy for Charlie.

Then in his senior year, Charlie went with the youth group to Haiti. First, there was the shock of abject poverty, worse than anything Charlie had ever seen, even in the ghettoes of his city back home. Then there was the incredible love and warmth of the Haitian people. The children constantly mobbing our van, hands outstretched for love or money or both. Even when they received no money, they were there, ready to kick a soccer ball, ready to smile, ready to make you feel as if maybe you really could make a difference in the world.

Then, there was the dysentery. Horrid pains. Diarrhea. Headaches. Not to mention the strange language, the strange food, and the added pressure of living in close community with the students in our group. By the evening sharing session on the fourth day of our trip, Charlie was broken. This guy, who everyone considered to have it all together, was reaching his limit.

Through his tears, he shared that in the last few days, he had come into a whole new awareness of who God is. For the first time in his life, he came to a point where he could move no further on his own. Neither charm, nor athletic ability, nor Mom and Dad could help him there in Haiti. He had to trust God. There was no other answer.

Paul Borthwick, who has for years utilized mission trips in the youth ministry at Grace Chapel in Lexington, Massachusetts, discusses in advance with his students the fact that, even with thorough planning, certain elements of the trip will be beyond their control. Whether it be the inherent danger of working in a crime-ridden inner-city neighborhood, or the ever present risk of picking up some bacterial infection in a strange place, he and his staff believe that the unplanned is what helps these students understand that this trip is in God's hands.

Paul recounts one episode in which a team of high-school students were working in a rural project in Africa that could only be reached by crossing a flooded stream. While the risk was acceptable, there was the possibility that the truck might get stuck in the stream, or worse, that in crossing the stream, the students might contract some bacterial infection through the water contact. Together, the team discussed the risks and the possibilities, and together they prayed for God's protection. Then, they went across. For those on the trip, it was a moment of God's faithfulness they will never forget.

It was the kind of moment that the average teenager, or the average youth worker, isn't going to experience during a normal week. And it happened because some youth workers dared to take these students out of their comfort zone so that they could see first-hand that God is faithful. (For more information on how to do youth mission trips, see Paul Borthwick's *Youth and Missions*, Sonpower/Victor, 1989.)

2. *Wilderness Trips*

It's possible that while reading the preceding paragraphs about stress and deprivation, you visualized a semi-cruel kind of manipulation by which we seek to brainwash a youth group. That is not the intent of these activities. What we are working with is the fact that for most American adolescents, a week without a video machine and a hair dryer amounts to deprivation of the severest sort. Watch a group of teenagers who live in the woods without mirrors, radios, pizzas, and television for a week, and you will see a group of teenagers under stress. That kind of real, but not cruel deprivation is what teenagers experience on a backpacking trip into the wilderness.

For that reason, backpacking is an excellent context in which to help students experience trust in God. The wilderness provides plenty of stress points for the average teenager. To begin with, living is carried on in new ways. Everything from setting up a tent to cooking a meal to going to the bathroom is new. Secondly, life in the wilderness is not easy. There are hills to contend with and packs to carry, and occasionally, rainy weather further complicates everything. It's not a pretty picture.

Then of course, there is the matter of living in close community—a community in which everyone is dependent on everyone else. And, in addition to all of the above, there is simply nature itself—this vast, sometimes mountainous, always awesome expanse of creation that somehow subtly reminds us of just how small we are in the grand scheme of things.

Carol, one of the girls in our group, was noting some of these very things in her journal the night she wrote: "I looked up today at all the beauty God had created. I try so hard to be pretty, and God, by his hand makes such beauty. I cried a little tonight as I thought about it. My mascara ran."

I once took a group of six high-school guys into Pinkham Notch, a huge wedge of mountain valley that borders the eastern slope of New Hampshire's Mount Washington. It was in the middle of winter, and we planned to climb up to Imp Face. These guys were fairly typical high-school males: cocky, self-sufficient, independent, and reluctant to admit that there might be an area of their lives in which they might have to admit to need.

We started our hike up the wall of the notch through eighteen inches of fresh snow. For most of us, it was the first time we had experienced walking in snowshoes. If it hadn't been so cold, and if the packs hadn't been so heavy with cold weather gear, it might have been funny. It took us over an hour to go the first one hundred yards.

By the end of our first mile, we struck humility. By that night, with a wind roaring louder than tandem freight engines, I found myself in a tent, hunkered in my sleeping bag, and talking to three high-school guys who were asking incredible questions about God. Out there in our little tent, sheltered from the biting winds, I could sense that these young men were beginning to come to grips with their need for faith in a very real, very big God. It was an evening I will long remember.

To be sure, it was scary. It was uncomfortable. But the fact is, without those conditions, the students might not have understood that, yes, even they needed God. (For more information about wilderness camping, backpacking, and using back country camping in youth ministry, see Eric Madsen's *Youth Ministry in the Wilderness*, Judson Press, 1982.)

3. *Rock Climbing/White Water Rafting*

A number of other kinds of activities put students under planned, abnormal stress that helps them come to terms with their personal faith in God. Experienced rock climbers often say that the rock is like a mirror, because it helps you to look more clearly and deeply into your own soul. Even with the proper equipment, and an experienced lead climber (two essentials), rock climbing can be an activity that takes students out of their comfort zone and into the faith zone.

Canoeing and white water rafting can also provide that same kind of opportunity. Again, certain safety measures must be observed, but even with the elimination of undue risk, this is a skill that is foreign enough to most kids that they will feel the squeeze of stress and uncertainty.

Elizabeth, a junior high girl, had been brought up in a Christian home with every advantage to learn about God and his sufficiency. But experiencing faith is difficult in a protected environment where it doesn't seem that God is necessary. I remember seeing Elizabeth disappear over a three-foot drop in the river as she charged the rapids in her "funyak." I suspect that, had her parents seen their little girl roaring down that river, they would have had me fired on grounds of negligence and insanity.

But I heard this sweet, proper little girl scream as she went over the falls, half with fear and half with exhilaration, and I watched as she looked back up the river from the eddy and flashed a big V with her fingers. And I heard her share that night that she had begun that day to discover that she and God could do things together that she hadn't dared to try before.

Youth workers can easily avail themselves of this kind of opportunity simply by finding the name of river outfitters in the area and then setting up a trip. If you do not know the names of any outfitters in your area, usually a backpacking or wilderness outfitter store is a good source of this kind of information. Or try the closest office of the National Forest Service.

4. *Ropes Course*

A growing number of camps and retreat centers are making use of ropes courses as a means by which students can push themselves to new limits and new vistas of trust. A ropes course is really nothing more than a high-altitude jungle gym of ropes, cables, and netting.

A typical ropes course might involve a trek across a tight-rope stretched between the tops of two trees, or a quick ride down a zip wire during which a student holds a wheel mechanism that runs down an extended length of cable. Some ropes courses use various configurations of suspended log bridges, tire swings, spider webbing made of climbing rope, or even a high wall with no footholds.

Silver Cliff Ranch in Buena Vista, Colorado has one element in their ropes course that features a high platform perched atop a lodgepole pine. And then, about six feet out is a trapeze to which one is supposed to jump. Even with the mandatory safety harness attached, it is a thought-provoking proposition.

Providing this kind of experience for a youth group gives them a wonderful opportunity to flesh out concepts like community, trust, and faith in very tangible ways. To set up this kind of activity, survey some of the camps in your area to see if they have a ropes course. On a wider scale, you may contact Christian Camping International (Box X, Wheaton, Illinois 60189) for the names of other camps and retreat centers that have a ropes course laid out.

We actually set up a very primitive version of a ropes course in the basement of our church building one Sunday night. Utilizing some of the more basic ropes course elements, we were still able to offer about five stations that gave students enough of a feel of difficulty that we were still able to accomplish our goal. (For more information about how to design and build a ropes course, see Karl E. Rohnke's *Cowstails and Cobras: A Guide to Leading Adventure Activities, Games, Group Initiative Problems, and Ropes Course Events*, published in 1989 by Project Adventure, P.O. Box 100, Hamilton, MA 01936.)

Essentially, any group can take advantage of the activities that have been suggested above. It is not necessary that either the students or the leaders be in top physical condition or that they be experienced North Woods guides. It is necessary to have proper safety equipment and proper leadership. If the youth leader is not proficient and experienced, the time and money spent to find and secure a good guide will be well worth it.

Building an intentionally stressful environment gives no excuse for poor planning or sloppy safety measures. There is a boundary beyond acceptable risk, and there have been youth leaders who have crossed that boundary only to encounter serious injury, lawsuits, and loss of credibility.

Anyone who is attempting to offer spiritual nurture to teenagers has got to be concerned about ways that we can increase their ability to survive the difficulties of living out a consistent and long-term commitment to Christ. For our kids to go the distance, they are going to have to be able to flesh out their faith in God. By utilizing some of the controlled stress situations that have been suggested above, we can help our students come to grips with their limits, and perhaps then come to realize the strength that we can draw from a faith in Christ, even under difficult conditions.

EXPERIENCE IS
THE BEST TEACHER

Several different kinds of purposeful and dramatized experiences can be incorporated to help teenagers flesh out their faith in concrete terms. Here are some broad categories with a few specific examples of each:

1. *Simulations*

To simulate is to create a situation that is lifelike, that is like something else. The idea is to allow our kids to experience in a learning situation what they may eventually have to experience in real life. This is an excellent teaching tool for helping kids explore their Christian faith in concrete terms.

Simulation games and activities are ignored by most of us in youth ministry. And yet simulation is probably the best way to help students learn through experience without having to pay too high a price for wrong decisions. John and Lela Hendrix quote an Air Force bomber pilot who said, "In twenty years as a pilot, I suffered only two major crises from which to learn. I lost two engines. Over the years, in the Link trainers and in more modern aircraft simulators, I have lost four engines, crashed twice and died once. Simulators offer some distinct advantages as environments in which to learn from experience" (*Experiential Education: X-Ed*, Abingdon Press, 1975).

There are certain lessons that simply aren't practical to teach our youth by means of direct experience. For example, World Vision came up with a program in the early eighties designed to heighten awareness of world hunger, while at the same time raising funds to feed those who are without. The Planned Famine concept has at its heart a thirty-hour fast that helps students in a very minimal way simulate some of the feelings and thoughts that accompany hunger. (For more information, write World Vision, Planned Famine, Box O, Pasadena, California 91109-9949.)

Another excellent example of material that uses simulation learning is The Compassion Project. Utilizing simulation games, music, Bible studies, and discussion starters, the creators of this project offer youth workers several different avenues to approach servant-hood. (Free from Compassion International, P.O. Box 7000, Colorado Springs, Colorado 80933).

To simulate a mission experience, the Jungle Aviation and Radio Service, the aviation wing of Wycliffe Bible Translators, has developed a simulation program called Jungle Jump-off. The idea behind the experience is to give youth groups a hint of what it might be like to live and work in a jungle outpost somewhere in the Amazon (contact JAARS, Waxhaw, North Carolina).

Sometimes a youth minister will want to use a simulation activity simply because it helps the students to learn in a more concrete way.

While giving a talk to students about community and body life, I wanted to emphasize the fact that we are one in Christ—what happens to one of us affects all of us. To simulate this kind of relationship, I had my students build a pyramid with their bodies. I challenged them to make it at least four levels high.

After about eight minutes of groaning, laughing, and instruction from many chiefs, they were able to build their pyramid. When the pyramid was disbanded we talked about what they had observed. Some students commented on the communication that was necessary to accomplish the task. Another observed that even the big guys on the bottom were very honest about expressing areas of need and discomfort(!).

One of the bottom level guys remarked that he was angry about how long it was taking to get everybody up, but he knew that if he abandoned his position, he would only cause himself a lot more pain when the pyramid caved in—and others would be hurt in the process. Another student observed that together they had built something that none of them alone could build. It was clear by our discussion, that through this simulation experience these students had learned some very vivid lessons about community. (For more information on this kind of activity see *Creative Teaching Methods*, Marlene Lefever: David C. Cook, and *Building Community in Youth Groups*, Denny Rydberg, Group Publishing, and *IDEAS Books*, Youth Specialties.)

2. *Games*

Sometimes we can help our students put flesh on their faith by playing games—not just games in which winning or losing is the key—but games in which value is placed more on what is learned through the competition. Sometimes these kinds of games are referred to as "initiative games" because they require from the group a certain kind of initiative if the group is going to be able to accomplish the goal of the game.

A good example of this kind of game is "Body Balloon Burst." In this game, students are assigned a body part based on the first letter of their last name, e.g. A-D = mouth, E-H = right hand, I-M = left hand, N-R = right foot, S-U = left foot, V-Z = rear end. When the game starts, each student will try to find five other people, each of a different body part, who can help them form a complete body with a mouth, two hands, two feet, and a rear end.

When the body is formed, the two legs carry one of the hands up to the front of the room where the hand is given a balloon. Then the feet carry the hand back to the group. The mouth blows up the balloon; the hands tie a knot in it. And then, the rear end sits on it and pops it. The first body to pop its balloon wins.

As a game, it is a lot of fun. But it is also an illustration of body life and the ministry of each part of the body, and it is an excellent example of experiential learning. Kids will sense the frustration of having too many mouths, or not enough feet, or no body through which they can exercise their part. It is critical in any instance of experiential learning such as this to give students time to discuss and process what they experience. (For more information about initiative games, see *Silver Bullets*, Project Adventure, South Hamilton, Massachusetts.)

3. *Role Playing*

In role play, students are assigned to various roles and told to act out the roles they are given. This may be a situation that involves an ethical question, or it may be a situation that allows students to view a situation from a new perspective. Role play allows students to face very difficult situations artificially, so that they will have a chance to think through their possible responses before facing the situation in real life.

A role play might involve two teenagers taking on the part of a father and son, with the father beginning the conversation by saying, "Why don't we communicate better?" Or it might be a role play in which two friends are pressuring a third friend to try drugs. Obviously, in terms of helping students to flesh out their faith in concrete terms, there are few activities more helpful than role play. (For more help in doing role plays, see *Creative Teaching Methods*, Marlene Lefever, David C. Cook, and *Roll-a-Role*, Youth Specialties. Also, some of the scenarios presented in *Tension Getters I and II* and *Amazing Tension Getters* can be used in role play situations.)

4. *Action Parables*

Action Parables are parables that have the added dimension of not only being heard, but being encountered. In that sense, they are multi-sensory. They are not just parables you hear, but parables you do.

An example of an action parable is the Truth Teller/Deceiver Walk. Students are assigned to teams of three. Two people on each team are designated guides, and the third person is designated the follower. Both designated guides are given the same destination. Then, at a signal, the teams make their way to the destination. The hitch is that in each team of three, one of the designated guides is a deceiver. The deceiver, using only his verbal persuasion tries to keep his team from reaching the destination first.

What happens is that the follower is forced to discern who is truthful and who is lying. Since both guides may be claiming to tell the truth, that is all the more difficult. A follower may decide simply to watch where other followers go, but he must realize that they could be misled. The game provides an interesting parable about how we decide which way to go, who we decide to listen to, and how we decide whom to trust.

MORE THAN JUST A PRETTY FAITH

The apostle Paul wrote to the church in Corinth, "The kingdom of God is not a matter of talk, but of power" (1 Corinthians 4:20). Helping students to nurture a concrete faith means that we are moving them from a faith that they talk about and know about, to a faith they experience. We may not feel comfortable standing on the cliff's edge, and we may hope that we will never find ourselves stuck in a rainstorm or camping in the mud. But by whatever means we use, we need to be sure we are giving students opportunities to learn about God from the neck down.

SECTION
THREE

THE PROCESS
OF NURTURE

CHAPTER THIRTEEN
REACH OUT AND TOUCH

"Philosophers have interpreted the world," Karl Marx once said. "The point is to change it." In youth ministry we aren't content with just defining teenage discipleship; we want to make it happen. That takes a long-term investment of nurture. Our mandate is to reach out and touch. We reach out to students to bring them into relationship with Christ. We help them to become strong and established in that relationship. Then we equip them to go out and reproduce that process of nurture in the life of another person. As Paul put it in 2 Timothy 2:2, "And the things you have heard me say in the presence of many witnesses entrust to reliable men who will also be qualified to teach others."

IT ALL BEGINS
WITH OUTREACH

A ministry of nurture must have arms wide enough to bring new kids into its embrace. Whether that wide reach entails Christian concerts, ski weekends, a day at the beach, an evening of bowling or a fifth quarter get-together after the Friday night game (events on what could be called a "Come join us" level), there must be some kind of context in which we have the opportunity to make contact and develop relationships with new kids. Somehow, it is our task to bring new kids from outside the ministry at least close enough to the ministry that they come within the realm of our influence. We cannot embrace those whom we cannot touch. And, we cannot touch kids' lives unless we first reach out.

SPENDING TIME
WITH KIDS

The one underlying characteristic of Jesus' ministry is that he was consistently in relationship with people. Whether he was confronting a prostitute by a well in the middle of a hot afternoon, or leading his closest followers in a time of prayer and special communion, it is clear that Jesus' ministry strategy was relational. He was not some aloof leader, dipping down in the jungle periodically like Tarzan to scream at and kick a few natives before he returned to his ruling roost in the treetops. In Jesus we see a God who became flesh and "made his dwelling among us" (John 1:14).

The core of any ministry of nurture is relationships. If our goal is to reach out and touch teenagers with the Gospel of Christ, we can do no less than our master. We need to get out among kids, go where they go, and put ourselves in situations in which we can build relationships with them. Some youth workers like to call this "contact work." A friend in Young Life likes to think of it as "intentional hanging out." If we want to make disciples, we must begin like Jesus did. Jesus went to where they were, whether it was the tax table or the fishing fleet, and he called them by name.

If we're completely honest, we would have to admit that this doesn't come easy for many of us. We look at ourselves in the mirror and realize that we are not one of "them"—and that they *know* we are not one of "them." As in the case of Jesus, we will probably find there is a cost to this kind of incarnational ministry. But it must be paid. Too many youth groups have used the Little Bo Peep method only to find that if we leave them alone these kids will not come back dragging their Bibles behind them.

On the other hand, building relationships with teenagers does not need to be as scary as we often make it out to be. To begin with, my experience in youth ministry has taught me that most teenagers are relationship-hungry. Granted, they do not go around seeking adults with whom they can bond. But if we take the risk of honestly reaching out to students where they are, with genuine love and acceptance, we will find some who respond.

Our problem is that most teenagers are suspicious of adults who want to get close to them. They are aware that most adults think of time spent among teenagers like time spent at the dentist. It will be painful, but it will eventually be over. However, my experience has been that when teenagers really believe that we have come to them with acceptance and concern, they usually respond.

Rod was one of those kids at the high school who had been branded by everyone as a metal-head, a burn-out, a freak. He did usually look like he had just awakened from sleep, and his dress was vintage Goodwill. He was one of the charter members in the high school's smoking area. I admit I wasn't exactly attracted to the guy at first.

I met him one day after having lunch at the high school. He asked me for a light (for his cigarette) and I handed him the flashlight from my glove compartment. He rolled his eyes and smiled, and I gave him a light from my car's cigarette lighter. He asked me what I was doing on campus, and we started a brief conversation.

I saw him off and on when I came on campus and I always made a point of seeking him out to say hello. Finally, I decided one day to ask him for some help on a Bible study I was doing about rock music. I asked him to bring over to my office some of his favorite tapes and tell me why people were so upset with this music. This guy must have brought half his music library. We played music and talked and played more music and talked.

I wish I could say that Rod eventually became a Christian and that he has since burned every rock-and-roll record he owns, but that wouldn't be true. And yet, Rod's story reminds us that we should not assume that every time we reach out to a student, we will be met with either complete rejection or miraculous conversion. Our job is not to make assumptions. Our job is to reach out and love people in Jesus' name.

TRY A
LITTLE KINDNESS

"How does it work?"

"What do I do?"

"If I went over to the high school, the kids would think I was a narc."

"I'm not cool enough or hip enough."

"I wouldn't know what to say."

Fear and discomfort are a very normal part of initiating any new relationship. It's especially understandable when we are reaching across cultures. And when we attend a basketball game with three teenage guys, or invite two teenage girls to go shopping with us, or bring a few kids over for dinner, make no mistake, we are doing cross-cultural ministry.

Like any cross-cultural ministry, this requires sensitivity, patience, determination, and compassion. In *The Youth Builder: A Resource for Relational Youth Ministry* (Harvest House, 1988), Jim Burns has some very helpful suggestions on how we might be more effective in contact work with teenagers. Drawing from some of his insights, let's consider the following suggestions:

1. *Remember names!*

This is the first and most important suggestion of all. In a world where people are identified by student numbers, social security numbers, or just "Hey, you!" teenagers appreciate it when someone remembers their name. Most of us excuse ourselves from this, because we aren't good at remembering names. But we can't get off the hook that easily. Remembering a name communicates something very special to a teenager.

Remembering names is a discipline. The more we work at it, the better we become at it. We can also utilize tricks of the trade, such as simply listening to kids refer to each other by name. I've been reminded of a student's name just by hearing their friend speak to them. Then, when I call the student by name, they are amazed that I bothered to remember.

Or sometimes I read the monogrammed name off of a letter jacket. It usually surprises a student when you call them by name and they forget that their name is on their jacket. "How did you know my name?" they ask. And I always say, "God told me." (Just be careful not to read the wrong name off the jacket. A kid may be offended if you greet him with "Hi, Fighting Ducks!")

Adult workers on the same ministry team should be encouraged to use students' names around each other. That clues in a leader who has had a slip of memory and helps to imprint that student's name in the memory. EXAMPLE: A leader walks over to another leader with the new student who visited last week and says, "Hey, Bill, did you see that Jake is back this week?" If that leader is on the ball, he can respond, "Oh yeah, Jake, how's it goin'?" And Jake is amazed that anybody remembers.

One youth minister tells of an encounter in which he was introduced to a person in his late twenties who identified himself as someone who had come to know Christ through this youth minister several years before. Obviously touched and encouraged by this discovery, the youth minister began to probe: "Please tell me how it happened. Was it a talk I gave? Was it something I did at a camp?"

"No," the stranger said. "You just remembered my name."

2. *Learn how to work through established relationships with students you know to meet new students you don't know.*

Plan special events to which youth-group kids can invite their friends. This is a very natural way for us to expand our embrace. Or sometimes if I am at a school event and I don't know a student, I will ask a student that I do know to introduce us. The next time, I will approach the student myself, and call him by name.

Don't be afraid to ask one of your regular kids the name of the student who came for the first time last week. I may be embarrassed that I've forgotten, but by asking one of my students for the visitor's name, I am not only getting information I need, I am modeling and demonstrating what it means to reach out and welcome newcomers to the group.

3. *Be an entrepreneur in servanthood.*

Brainstorm about ways that you can serve teenagers that you know in your community. Sometimes this can be done on an individual level by volunteering to tutor, to chaperone at a school event, to coach a team, or to drive a van for a sports team. Or it may done on a wider level. One youth minister, for example, reaches out to kids in the community with a Caught in the Middle seminar for students who come from families that have experienced a divorce.

4. *Don't try to be a teenager.*

There is nothing more pathetic than a thirty-year-old adult trying to act like a fifteen-year-old kid. Not only is the wrong message portrayed about how we should approach our own growth and maturity, but this usually comes off as phoney and weird. I can remember when I was a teenager in the late sixties, occasionally being approached at a church gathering by some forty-year-old hippie with beads and long hair who wanted to rap with us. It was all we could do to stifle the laughter.

Teenagers do not need or expect adults to act like teenagers. What they do need, but generally don't expect, is for adults to be comfortable around teenagers acting like teenagers. Typically, they have learned that if they want to be accepted by an adult, they must not act like a teenager—no jeans, no music, no fooling around.

Adults who spend time with teenagers tend to make one of two mistakes: either they try to be peers, or they seem to come off as parents. Teenagers do not need more peers. They have all the peers they need. Likewise they do not need additional parents. I have never yet met a teenager who has said, "You know, if I just had a couple more parents I'd be in great shape." Our role is to be neither a peer, nor a parent, but to be a priest and a pastor—one who stands between those kids and God and tries to bring them together.

5. *Use the SLIR approach.*

Many times our fear is based on the simple fact that we aren't sure what to talk about when we're with teenagers. They don't seem to be interested in taxes, investments, politics, recipes, homemaking tips, or other important topics adults like to discuss. And we feel silly and uninformed talking about the latest album by New Kids on the Block.

Veteran youth worker Les Christie uses the acrostic SLIR to help his volunteers initiate conversations with new kids they meet at youth-group activities or while doing contact work. His suggestion:

    S = **School**—Ask questions about school: i.e. what grade they're in, classes they like, classes they don't like, etc.

    L = **Likes**—Ask for opinions about music, movies, etc.

    I = **Interests**—How do they enjoy spending free time?

    R = **Religion**—What are their thoughts about God? Who is Jesus?

Some youth workers have actually designed simple sheets that help leaders think through in advance the conversations that they need to have with particular students. While this may seem stilted, phoney, or just too mechanical, this makes much more sense than sitting through an entire conversation with a kid and talking about nothing deeper than the last movie he saw or the last record she heard.

That isn't to suggest that every conversation and every contact must have deep spiritual content, but it seems reasonable to suggest that very busy leaders who finally nail down an opportunity to spend some time with very busy students might want to spend a few minutes thinking in advance about what they would like to ask or share or accomplish in this encounter.

A sample of such a sheet is below. It is used on occasion by members of the adult leadership team for student ministry at Church of the Savior in Wayne, Pennsylvania.

PERSON-TO-PERSON SHEET

Student's Name _____ Date _____

Share Jesus —Verses, OT thoughts, etc. —Get a sense of his/her devotional life, or relationship with Christ.

Share Hearts —Confession, struggles, joys, etc. —Develop transparency

Talk Over Expressed Needs —Things he/she desires, areas of mutual concern

Edify —Give positive affirmation—Express gratitude to him/her

Determine/Discuss Needs and/or Goals:
  • in relationship to God
  • in relationship with others
  • in the ministry

Responsibilities/Tasks/Projects

Other

Some have suggested that teenagers might be offended if they thought that an adult had been forced to plan their supposedly informal conversation. That may be true. But I don't think there has been one person today that actually spent time thinking about how they could make their conversation with me the most spiritually uplifting and helpful conversation it could be. And if I found out that someone was taking that kind of time for me I would: (1) be very impressed that someone would care that much about my spiritual welfare; (2) make sure that I spent some time with that person!

Sometimes we can facilitate that relational time by DOING something with a student better than we can by actually sitting down across a table with an appointment to TALK ABOUT something. Again, there are those who aren't sure what kinds of things we can do with an adolescent that they will consider fun. We sense, rightly perhaps, that the average teenager is not going to get goose bumps at the thought of an afternoon with an adult. On the other hand, we shouldn't underestimate how much teenagers appreciate the time and attention shown by an adult who is willing to stop all of the usual busy-ness of being an adult long enough to share life with them.

Below is a list of suggestions that might spark some thinking about how an adult leader can spend time with a teenager.

THIRTY THINGS YOU CAN DO WITH A KID

1. Coke and a Smile (Just sit down over a Coke).
2. Do a photo essay of other kids' rooms/or the kid's own room.
3. Make a video.
4. Throw a frisbee.
5. Throw a party.
6. Go to a professional/college sporting event.
7. Have devotions together (read Bible and pray together).
8. All night Monopoly/Pictionary/Trivial Pursuit (NOTE: All night events probably work better with people of the same sex).
9. Go bowling.
10. Go skating.

11. Fly to Libya together.
12. Work together on a building project for Habitat for Humanity or do some other one day/one afternoon service project together.
13. Go to a school event (there's always something going on), preferably not just a popular activity. If you show up at the oboe recital, you WILL be noticed!
14. Go to a movie or rent a video.
15. Go rock climbing/hiking/cross-country skiing.
16. Ride bikes.
17. Ride zeppelins.
18. Ask the teenager to teach you how to use your computer.
19. Build a model.
20. Work on a mural for the youth room.
21. Go to the mall.
22. Set up a perfect date for the kid's friend (prepare dinner, chauffeur them around, wait on them).
23. Tutor the kid in a subject he is struggling with.
24. Take him to visit a college he's thinking about attending.
25. Make a birthday cake for one of the other kids in the youth group.
26. Wash a car together (preferably yours; maybe theirs).
27. Practice your Boy Scout knots.
28. Work through a Bible study book together.
29. Write a song together.
30. Stay up all night and watch a meteor shower together (the best showers are after midnight).

Aside from one-on-one activities, there are, of course, hundreds of ideas for reaching out to unchurched students through various recreational and social activities (For a good sampling of ideas, see Rice and Yaconelli's *Creative Socials and Special Events*, Youth Specialties/Zondervan, 1986). Traditionally, this has been one of the main ways that youth groups have reached out to their community, and that's great. Jesus took time to minister to the large masses, even feeding several thousand people on a few occasions.

We make a mistake though, when we allow a large group activity to take the place of person-to-person contact. Rarely do teenagers have such a great Food Frolic down at the church that they somehow decided to give their lives to Christ. We must continually remind ourselves and our leaders that even the large group activities are simply to provide a context in which we can initiate and build relationships with individual students.

Art Erickson, one of the real veterans of youth ministry, has been working with students in urban Minneapolis for more than twenty years. One of the marks of Art's ministry has been a heavy emphasis on relationships. A few years ago, his church in Minneapolis, Park Avenue United Methodist Church, decided to host a special celebration of Art's ministry through the years. As a part of that ministry, some of Art's former youth-group kids were invited to write letters of appreciation that would be presented to Art as a part of the celebration of his faithful ministry.

The following letter, submitted by one of Art Erickson's youth-group alumni, epitomizes the importance and the rewards of a ministry that reaches and touches students' lives.

Another way I would put it is something I've always thought when I thought about you. You were a guy who never slept in the counselor's tent. The counselor's tent is the place where the grown-ups go to get away from the kids, where they go to recoup their sanity after a long day spent with us, where they go to shut us out, and where they go to talk grown-up talk with each other, play cards, and have a good time. I always felt a little lonely when the counselors were in their tent. I often wondered about this one particular and peculiar counselor who for some odd reason decided that he liked the noise and the moldy smell in our tent more than he liked the camaraderie, quiet cleanness, and adultness that resided in the counselor's tent.

I had a hunch that you might enjoy getting away, but for some weird reason, you didn't. You were there in our tent, when I was twelve, talking with us about sex and girls and what real love was about when other adults thought we didn't think about stuff like that at our age.

You were there in our tent when I was thirteen and had just become a Christian, and was somewhat awkwardly putting on the new clothes of a relationship with Christ. You were there in my tent when I was fifteen and struggled with the painful and awkward feelings about whether I was lovable or not.

You were there in our tent when I was eighteen and out on a Colorado desert in the middle of nowhere when we were all too tired after walking twenty miles to care much about anything.

You were there when I was twenty and inwardly confused and fed up with my image as a "good Christian"—when I smashed the window of a car as an expression of my unrecognizable anguish inside. You stayed in my tent through all that stuff.

I often wondered about that habit you had of sleeping in our tent, even though the stuff in there wasn't that neat or pretty or clean. I guess I've now found out why you chose to do that, and what it meant.

THE TWO MOST COMMON QUESTIONS

Usually when youth leaders are presented with the challenge and opportunity of doing relational outreach with teenagers, they respond with some form of these two generic questions:

Question #1—How am I supposed to find time to do all that this kind of ministry entails when I have a family, a job, and other responsibilities?

First comes the bad news. Jesus was a busy person. Being the Savior of the world, the Master Teacher, and Great Physician is equally as time-consuming as any tasks that we face. And yet he spent, conservatively, twelve hours a day over a three-year-period with a group of twelve disciples. That multiplies out to about 4,300 hours a year that he spent with these people. Since most of us in youth work might spend, at the most, seven hours a week with a student (counting Bible study, youth group and some kind of activity), it would take us approximately thirty-six years to garner that kind of time with a student. And unless we are speaking of a very poor student, we will not have them in the high-school group that long!

But the good news is that something is better than nothing. We may not be able to pour our lives into twenty students for three to seven hours a week on an individual basis. But we can pour one hour into one student every week, meeting maybe for a breakfast, or during a study hall, or on a Saturday morning. And we should not underestimate the impact that even that kind of consistent attention can have in a student's life. We mustn't forget that if we are spending even one hour a week with that student, we are probably spending one hour more per week with that student than any other adult they know, including, possibly, their parents.

"WHY AREN'T WE REACHING MORE KIDS?"

Question #2—If we have been having outreach events and trying to build relationships with new students, why aren't we bringing in any new kids?

Obviously there could be many reasons why a group might find its outreach much shorter and more ineffective than it would like. There are as many reasons as there are groups. But to make a long answer short, consider these realities. The church's outreach typically fails because of blandness, bluntness, blunders, and blindness.

Blandness

One of the reasons that non-churched students are unmoved by our outreach events is that the closer they get to us, the more they see that we are just like them. We talk about a supernatural love and a special kind of community, but that is not always what newcomers experience when they come to our group. When the outsiders looked on at the church in Acts 2 they saw a quality about them that they could not explain. Drawing from their only frame of reference, they assumed, "They have had too much wine" (Acts 2:13). I am not sure that newcomers sense that same kind of inexplicable joy and fellowship in many of our churches and youth groups.

We are talking about blandness: teaching that simply isn't as creative as it might be; games that are not quite as much fun as they could be if someone took some extra creative effort; food that seems to have been prepared with the idea that, "Well, it's only teenagers so it doesn't matter"; fellowship that isn't marked by warmth and acceptance; in short, just a general lack of excellence.

We often excuse this blandness because our hearts are in the right place. But if we want to reach out to unchurched teenagers we will have to earn the right to be heard. That doesn't mean that we have to offer a lavish evening that rivals prom night. It does mean that we can settle for nothing less than our best effort at creativity, planning, promotion, and general excellence for Christ.

I have always been impressed with the way Young Life hosts its week-long summer camps. These camps are intentionally evangelistic. They are designed to appeal to and embrace unchurched, non-Christian teenagers. Young Life tells these students in advance that it will be the best week of their lives. And it often is.

From the moment the students arrive at the site of departure for camp to the time they arrive back to the parking lot to be picked up after camp, every effort has been made to win for adult leaders the right to be heard. The facilities are excellent, apparently designed with the question, "How can we make this as much fun as possible for a teenager?" as opposed to "How cheaply can we get by given that we need to save most of our budget for the adult facility across the highway?"

The food is creatively prepared and tasty. The counselors see their role as building relationships, not policing the kids and protecting the property. And for the nightly messages, rather than bringing in some denominational official to whom the camp must show homage, there is a communicator who knows how to make the Gospel alive and relevant to the unchurched teenager. Teenagers who have never been to church find themselves saying by the end of the week, "There is something different here: these people, their attitude, their joy, their love. Maybe what they are saying about Jesus is true."

I know about this because I was one of those kids. I became a Christian through just that kind of camp experience.

Bluntness

Then of course there is the matter of bluntness: saying the right things in the wrong way so that we turn off and offend our visitors. Granted, there is a fine line between backing off of the Gospel and being sensitive to one's audience. But I am impressed with the fact that some people have enough of a relational basis with their audience, or such an ability to communicate love, that they can say some very hard things to people, and the people keep coming back for more. This is a ministry skill that we all must cultivate if we are going to be effective in outreach.

An entry in the journal of the great British preacher John Wesley gives an example of this kind of ability.

We came to Bolton about five in the evening. We had no sooner entered the main street than we perceived the lions at Rochdale were lambs in comparison to those (here) at Bolton. Such rage and bitterness I scarcely ever saw before in creatures that bore the form of men. [Does this sound like a junior-high lock-in to you?] They followed us in full cry to the house where we went; and as soon as we had gone in, took possession of all the avenues to it and filled the street from one end to the other.

After some time the waves did not roar so loud. Mr. P. thought he might then venture out. They immediately closed in, threw him down and rolled him in the mire; so that when he scrambled from them and got into the house again, one could scarcely tell what or who he was. When the first stone came among us through the window, I expected a shower to follow; and the rather, because they had now procured a bell to call their whole forces together. But they did not design to carry on the attack at a distance: presently one ran up and told us the mob had burst into the house: he added, that they had got J. B. in the midst of them. They had, and he laid hold on the opportunity to tell them of the "terrors of the Lord" [I'll bet he did].

Meanwhile, D.T. engaged another part of them with smoother and softer words. Believing the time was now come, I walked down into the thickest of them. They had now filled all the rooms below. I called for a chair. The winds were hushed, and all was calm and still. My heart was filled with love, my eyes with tears, and my mouth with arguments. They were amazed; they were ashamed; they were melted down; they devoured every word.

We must somehow communicate to our students that we can disapprove of their sin and their lifestyle without disapproving of them. I have been in some Christian camps and rallies in which a teenager would have to be a Christian before they came or they would not have tolerated all of the extra rules, regulations, and expectations.

I spoke at one youth outreach event in Pennsylvania in which the youth pastor of the host church where the event was being held stood up to speak the first night, and with the first words out of his mouth he told the kids, "Last year, when we had this event, somebody went into the boys room and urinated on the walls; we're not going to have that this year." You could just sense that the kids were all thinking, "Wow, this sounds like it's going to be fun!"

Paul spoke in 1 Thessalonians about what I think must have been the key to his tremendous ministry of outreach. "We loved you so much that we were delighted to share with you not only the Gospel of God but our lives as well, because you had become so dear to us" (1 Thessalonians 2:8). How many times have teenagers been turned off by well-meaning believers because our bluntness mistakenly communicated a desire to share our message, but not our lives?

Blunders

Thirdly, we need to be warned of blunders that sometimes sabotage our outreach efforts, mistakes that we make due to inexperience or lack of training. One youth minister in our area was so eager to reach out to kids that she planned a big one-night youth rally. That was okay. But in her zeal to make it a great evening, she had planned so many different parts of the program that the evening seemed to last forever. First there was the thirty minutes of sing-a-long, then the local Christian rock band sang for forty minutes. Then there were various skits, a testimony, more sing-a-long, a short Christian film, and then another testimony. By the time I got up to give what was supposed to have been an evangelistic message, the only kids left in the auditorium were a few Christian kids praying that their ride would still be waiting at the church when the van got back to the parking lot. Good intentions, but a serious blunder.

Blindness

Finally, let's remember that when it's all said and done, even if it's all said creatively and all done right, we still will not be effective with every student. After all, we are doing outreach ministry; we are literally trying to help spiritually blind people see the light of Christ. That is a work that involves much more than having the pizza arrive on time and the gym open. This is a spiritual enterprise that can only be successful as spiritually blind teenagers are open to the guidance of God's Spirit. That means we need to bathe the whole operation with prayer.

THE BOTTOM LINE

Despite the blunders, the bluntness, the blandness, and the blindness, God is able to work through ministries just like ours. When he does, it is because we have taken the time to love people, to reach out and touch them. Even when we do a lot of things wrong, God's love through us can make very good things happen.

CHAPTER FOURTEEN

ENCOURAGING NEW GROWTH AND GROWING NEW ENCOURAGERS

About a year ago I found myself in a Toronto hotel that was hosting a coaches' convention sponsored by NIKE Sportswear. My partner and I, both avid fans of college basketball, had the whole Friday night free so we decided we would sit in on some of the sessions. We knew our plans had been inspired that night when the main speaker was introduced for the evening session: "Folks, let's welcome from North Carolina State University the head basketball coach, Jim Valvano."

Valvano, head coach of college basketball's championship team just five seasons ago, was in rare form that night as he told the audience of coaches that the one absolute necessity for winning is to have a goal. For some coaches, the goal may be as modest as winning one game or just having a winning season. For Valvano, it was clear, his goal was to coach a second, national-championship basketball team. But he went on that evening to say that a goal alone is not enough. It takes more than a goal. And it was that thought that challenged me.

Any sports fan knows that there are three essential elements for a consistent winning effort. One is a goal. That's important. Two is a plan. That makes sense. But third, and all important, is execution. Nothing happens without execution. If you've ever watched your favorite sports team run for the wrong goal or demonstrate a sloppy game plan, you probably couldn't help but sit there, staring at your television screen, and think about execution (in more ways than one).

As we move through this final section of the book, we want to talk specifically about how to execute the kind of ministry that will nurture teenagers in their walk with Christ.

The following diagram, loosely adapted from a similar layout originally developed in *Youth Ministry Resources* (Vol. 3, U.S. Catholic Conference, Department of Education, 1979), provides for us a helpful framework for thinking about the actual execution of a ministry of nurture.

Outreach	Nurture	Equipping	
Come-Level Events/ Contact Work	Community Building	Teaching	Service

(a) Spending Time With Them . . . .
(b) Modeling Christ . . . .
(c) Help Them Establish
and Deepen Their Commitment to God. . . . .
(d) Call Them to Service . . . .

Relationship Building	Relationships/Content	Delegation	

This diagram illustrates the three essential elements of any effective on-going ministry of nurture: outreach, nurture, and equipping for service. In our last chapter, we focused on outreach. Our emphasis in this chapter is on nurturing, helping new believers get established in the faith so that they can begin to grow and reach out to others.

NURTURING FOR THE FUTURE

There is an intriguing incident in the early chapters of 2 Kings (2 Kings 2:9–14) in which the prophet Elisha is saying a final good-bye to his mentor and beloved friend, Elijah. These two men of God had seen a lot together, but both of them knew that it was time for them to go their separate ways. Crossing over the Jordan River,

Elijah said to Elisha, "Tell me, what can I do for you before I am taken from you?"

"Let me inherit a double portion of your spirit," Elisha replied.

"You have asked a difficult thing," Elijah said, "yet if you see me when I am taken from you, it will be yours—otherwise not."

As they were walking along and talking together, suddenly a chariot of fire and horses of fire appeared and separated the two of them, and Elijah went up to heaven in a whirlwind. Elisha saw this and cried out, "My father! My father! The chariots and horsemen of Israel!" And Elisha saw him no more. Then he took hold of his own clothes and tore them apart.

He picked up the cloak that had fallen from Elijah and went back and stood on the bank of the Jordan. Then he took the cloak that had fallen from him and struck the water with it. "Where now is the Lord, the God of Elijah?" he asked. When he struck the water, it divided to the right and to the left, and he crossed over.

What is especially moving about that passage, I believe, is the obvious pain that both Elijah and Elisha felt about their parting. Elisha had learned so much from this great man of God, that it must have been difficult to imagine carrying on the ministry and the work without the support and encouragement of that relationship. I doubt if either Elijah or Elisha wanted to let go, and yet they both sensed that this was God's leading (2 Kings 2:1–6).

I see a picture of youth ministry in that episode, some parts of it obvious, some not so obvious. The obvious part is that Elisha, the great prophet of God, was bald-headed. But beyond that, I see in this story the mixture of satisfaction and uneasiness that a lot of us feel when we see students graduate from the youth program each year and move on to a new post-high-school, post-youth-group era of life. We have come to love these people. We have prayed for them, played with them, and probably gotten angry with them on occasion.

But now it is all said and done. They have come to a point when they are no longer under our direction. They are no longer within the realm of our care and influence. And that's not always so easy to accept. Sooner or later, we will all know the bittersweet experience of seeing our Elishas cross the river by themselves, with the full realization that from this point they are on their own. The question at that point will be for these kids, as it was for Elisha, how effectively have we reproduced ourselves in the lives of our students? How effectively have we nurtured their personal walk with Christ?

The process of Christian nurture is the process whereby youth leaders attempt to transfer their vision, their values, their wisdom, and their experience to a new believer. It would be simple enough if our students could just inherit, in the words of Elisha, a double portion of our spirit (2 Kings 2:9). But it isn't that easy. Elijah's assessment was, "You have asked a difficult thing." Difficult or not, one of the major tasks of a ministry of nurture is helping new believers to become established in the faith so that they can walk with the Lord on their own.

The last Sunday in the evening service at Barrington (Rhode Island) Baptist Church was one of those river crossings for me. This had been my very first full-time youth-ministry position. And now, after four years, I was moving to a new position in another part of the country. There was a closing circle of prayer as our church family ringed the sanctuary, and then at the close of the service, a receiving line to say a final good-bye to these dear friends. Hugging and crying with those students I had come to love was an extremely tough experience.

I had confidence in the leaders we were leaving behind. I knew that God had done a substantial work in the lives of many of these kids. But still, there was that sense that each of those kids carried a part of me with them, and vice-versa. And I think we all knew that after that evening I would not see most of them ever again.

Now, about ten years later, I look back on that evening with all the pride of a builder going back to his first construction project. Because now, after ten years, I have heard reports about many of those very students, and the miracle is they're still standing. Sheri is working as a missionary in China. Carla and her husband are actively serving their church as lay people in New Hampshire. Dave is an active member of a congregation in California. Hans is just finishing up his studies in youth ministry so that he can do some kind of mission work with teenagers.

Exciting stuff, but it didn't just happen. It required effective execution of a ministry of nurture.

THE MASTER'S PLAN

I was fresh out of seminary when I read Robert Coleman's *The Master Plan of Evangelism* (Revell, 1978), a classic study of Jesus' ministry among his twelve disciples. To this day, the insights of that book shape many of my notions about youth ministry and my philosophy of ministry. In the book, Coleman studies the life and ministry of Jesus with his followers so that we might be able to utilize that same plan as we work with our own disciples. It is an open window to Jesus' own ministry of nurture. By combining and re-shaping some of Coleman's insights, we can discover four basic steps in the Master's Plan for nurture: spend time with them, model your faith, help them to establish and deepen their commitment to God, and release and commission them to reproduce themselves spiritually.

1. *Spend Time With Them.*
    We've already observed in the preceding chapter that any Christlike approach to ministry is going to involve relationships. Jesus' mission and ministry revolved around people. Most of us in youth ministry are quite aware that teenagers need lots of time and love. Nurture can't be done at a distance. And yet we struggle because we sense that there is a limit to how many quality relationships we can genuinely maintain. How do we know which students to nurture?

WHICH KIDS WILL I NURTURE?

Steve was in his first youth-ministry position. With his love for kids, his contagious faith, and healthy sense of fun, he found himself almost immediately overrun with students. The growth in his group was remarkable. But Steve had enough sense to realize that a ministry that was wide but not deep was not going to leave a lasting impression on these teenagers. When he came to me, he was concerned about how he could nurture the students that seemed interested in growth, without alienating the students who were simply along for the ride.

Obviously, we talked about the importance of team ministry, and we talked about the fact that a deep ministry with a few students can ultimately impact more kids than a shallow ministry with a lot of students. But having said all of that, it still came down to the fact that, like Jesus, Steve would have to be willing to choose a few students with whom he would spend the bulk of his quality time. We both knew that wouldn't be easy; it would require wisdom and discernment.

We need to remember that Jesus called to himself twelve. He spent time out among the masses, loving and caring for those who, perhaps, showed no immediate spiritual promise at all. But he poured his life into twelve men. Paul had his small band that he traveled with. Elijah had his Elisha. As youth ministers, we cannot allow ourselves to feel guilty about selecting a few students to whom we will try to give extra time and training.

Youth ministers who are not willing to do this usually end up sacrificing depth in their ministry for fear of offending the students who aren't presently motivated to grow. In short, we tend to gear each youth-ministry activity to the lowest common spiritual denominator. If we sense that we can have a few more kids at Bible study by watering down the content, we will water down the content. But in so doing, we are neglecting the nurture of those few kids at Bible study who are seriously seeking spiritual nourishment.

We can make the choice to do that. But that's when we have to ask ourselves who and what is going to be left behind when we cross to the other side of the river. If we are not nurturing some Elishas in our ministry, then we run the risk of leaving a ministry that has all impact of an ice cube in hot tea. We might have some minor impact that way, but the only lasting impression is going to be lukewarm.

So how do we know which students to nurture? One way is to allow these students to identify themselves. If I am going to have a team of leadership students that I involve in various tasks of leadership in my ministry, then I will begin by making it clear that involvement on the team is an option open to every student. However, to be involved on the leadership team there are certain requirements, some involving time, some involving various spiritual disciplines, etc. In other words, if a student looks beyond the requirements and says, "I want to be on the team," that student is identifying himself as a potential Elisha.

I would also seek out certain students that I felt should be on that team and challenge them to consider being involved. Jesus called his disciples by name. We should be bold enough to say to a student, "You know, Brenda, I think you ought to pray about being on this leadership team. It would be a great way for the Lord to use you in this ministry." I have worked with students who, without my initiation and encouragement, might not have considered themselves Elisha material. But with my invitation, they got plugged into the program, and they had wonderful ministries.

But what kind of students do we seek out? The Navigators use a little three letter acrostic to describe the kind of person that seems to benefit the most from personal ministry: FAT. They suggest that if our aim is to effectively nurture a new believer, we should look for FAT Christians—those who are *F*aithful, *A*vailable, and *T*eachable.

Faithful. The first priority of a nurture relationship is that the student be faithful to God. If a student lacks a genuine commitment, then the time invested in nurture is going to be less profitable than it could be. That doesn't mean that we invest no time in the student. It does mean that as adult leaders who have a very clear vision and very real limitations on our time, and we may have to exercise discretion about how and with whom we invest the time we have. That may sound cold-blooded to some, but if we can look beyond our messianic need to be needed, we can also see that there are many different ways and people through whom God can reach a student. Sometimes, what looks like indifference may just be the back-side of wise stewardship.

I had one guy in my first youth ministry who was constantly wanting to spend time with me. He would call me every night, come by several afternoons a week, and hang out at my house as much or more than I did. At first, being new in youth ministry, I was flattered. I thought it was neat that the kid actually liked me. It didn't bother me that he never seemed to make any movement closer to Christ. I felt that our time together was giving me a platform from which to share my faith. And it was.

But after awhile, I began to realize that the time I was investing in Don was taking me away from other relationships with students who might seriously want to grow and who might, given a little extra time, really bear some spiritual fruit. In short, though Don was Available, he was not Faithful, and I had to focus less time on Don and more time on other students.

Available. In this day when students are so busy with a myriad of activities, availability is becoming more and more of a problem. We cannot nurture someone with whom we have no contact. Often it is the students who are the most faithful spiritually, who are the least available because they are the type of student who understands commitment. Everyone wants a piece of their action.

I had an incredible experience recently when I sauntered up to a high-school student to see if we could get together over the next week. When I tried to nail him down on a time, he pulled out of his back-pocket a Daytimer calendar. Feeling a little stunned by this brash, atypical display of adolescent organization, I asked the student, "Bobby, what is that?"

He responded, "Oh, it's my Daytimer. It helps me keep things organized with soccer, student council, stuff for youth group, and things that are happening at home. It's great," he volunteered. "You ought to get one." The good news is that he was able to work me in later that week.

Looking for students who are available to be nurtured is only common sense. Genuine discipleship takes time. If a student doesn't have that kind of time, it does not mean that they are being unfaithful. It just means that for that time, they cannot realistically add any new commitments into their schedule.

Students, however, need to be challenged about how they spend their time, and about the choices they have made about which activities they will be involved in. A particular student may need to be nurtured more than he needs to be in the band. And if it comes down to one or the other, students should be allowed/forced to deal with that issue.

Again, availability can best be assessed by simply being candid about time commitments required for a particular discipleship program. If there is a time commitment, stick to that commitment. Students who are not available will generally eliminate themselves.

Teachable. It stands to reason that even if a student is both faithful and available, if he is unteachable, he is not going to benefit greatly from extra teaching. I have worked with some students who soaked up every insight and responded positively to every correction, and I have worked with others who were either hyper-sensitive about correction or too arrogant to learn. A student who is genuinely open, with a sincere desire to grow and learn, is a rare and precious find. God can use a teachable heart.

ONE-ON-ONE
MINISTRY

Both Jesus and Paul must have spent much time in one-on-one ministry with their followers. Mark 3:14 specifically states, "He appointed twelve—designating them apostles—that they might be with him and that he might send them out to preach." Those who have been involved in youth ministry for very long know well the importance of having this kind of time with students. I have known teenagers who exhibited all of the vitality of a terminal coma when they were among their friends, but when alone in one-on-one conversations, they were open to discussing deep spiritual truth.

As we begin to identify students with whom we feel we can have deeper spiritual input, we need to involve them progressively in two different types of relationships—a relationship of nurture and a relationship of ministry (in which they are beginning to assume some responsibility for another person's spiritual growth). Youth minister Jackson Crum helps his students and adult leaders think in these terms by using the following chart.

ESSENTIAL
RELATIONSHIPS

Who's Loving You	You	Friend or Two at School

He builds some accountability into this approach by keeping a notebook that helps him to track which students and leaders are spending time together, and what kinds of conversations and issues they are sharing in their time together. Every week, adult leaders and leadership students turn in what is fondly referred to as a People Sheet.

PEOPLE SHEET

Who have you been with?

How/When were you with them?

What did you hope to accomplish?

Specific prayer need for that person:

On the back side of a People Sheet are the following questions to help leaders think about contacts with other students.

Who do you need to be with?

When have you planned to be with them?

What needs to happen during the time?

While this may strike some people as too mechanical, or needless paperwork, it may be that it will take just this kind of intentional effort to make sure that every student is involved in some kind of nurture relationship. Jesus' disciples numbered only twelve. Accountability may not have been difficult. But for us, as our youth group grows, we need to be careful that every student is getting some individual touch on a weekly basis. Unfortunately, it is the ugly-duckling kid, or the student who is kind of quiet, or maybe just the average student who doesn't cause much trouble, who usually gets neglected.

2. *Model Your Faith*

As Jesus' disciples spent time with Jesus, they were constantly learning about a relationship with God, sometimes through teaching, often simply by watching Jesus model a life of obedience and intimate fellowship. It's fun to note how closely the disciples followed Jesus' example, especially when they were in a clutch situation. In Acts 4:1–11, Peter and John found themselves in particularly difficult circumstances as they were confronted by the elders, rulers, and teachers from the synagogue. They were questioning John's and Peter's basis of authority for their preaching.

As one reads the text, one can almost hear John and Peter saying, "Well, what would the Master say in a case like this? What did he say when they nailed him with this kind of stuff?" And sure enough, in Acts 4:11 they cite a rather obscure verse from Psalm 118, "The stone you builders rejected . . . has become the capstone." One might ask, where did they get that verse? But if we read back in Matthew 21:42, that is precisely the verse Jesus used in defending himself against the same kind of charges. Jesus never said, "Now, if you're in a tight spot, here's a neat verse you can use." They learned by his example.

Likewise the Apostle Paul could refer to his own lifestyle when he wrote to the church at Philippi because he modeled the gospel he preached. "Join with others in following my example, brothers, and take note of those who live according to the pattern we gave you" (Philippians 3:17).

Modeling is one of the major reasons that we must spend time with our students. By being with them in good situations and bad situations, wonderfully worshipful situations and mundanely normal situations, we give them a chance to see what it looks like to be a disciple of Jesus. This kind of modeling has always been one of the key ways that disciples have been nurtured. As Peter put it, "To this you were called, because Christ suffered for you, leaving you an example, that you should follow in his steps" (1 Peter 2:21).

What that means is that when we are with students, we needn't always be "teaching" them about the Christian life. For example: the two of you are throwing a frisbee together and a bad throw hits an elderly lady in the head as she walks by. That is not your cue to call the student over and say, "You know, the Bible says that sin is like that. We miss the mark, and it causes pain—someone gets hurt." Modeling takes place when they see us in our homes with our families, when they watch us deal with a cashier at the mall, when they hear us talk through decisions we must make.

A WORD OF CAUTION

One of the important cautions at this point is that we must make sure that we are modeling with the intent to help students be like Jesus — not to help them be like us. We are called to disciple students, not clone them. It is all too easy to make the mistake of thinking that if these students were really faithful and teachable, they would be exactly like us. They would have our tastes in music, in clothes, in hair style, etc. Or that if they were really faithful to our model, they would go to the same Christian college we went to, or share the same vocational goals or political views. Despite the fact that we are flattered by students who mimic our mannerisms and life patterns, we need to remember that our mission is to draw attention to Jesus and not to ourselves.

Sometimes this unhealthy mimicking happens just because teenagers want so much to be like us. If we are outgoing, they feel they must be. If we are athletic, they feel they must be.

Unfortunately that kind of cloning can lead to real problems. Sometimes students emulate us to such a degree that they emulate even our weaknesses. They model us so completely that they model even those parts of our life that are not Christ-like.

In my earliest years of youth ministry, I really didn't talk much about missions and caring for the poor. I didn't mean to neglect this important element of the Great Commission. I was just immature. Sad to say I think to some extent I reproduced that same kind of attitude in many of the students with whom I worked.

Teenagers are very impressionable, very susceptible to manipulation by our modeling. We need to realize that kids often watch our behavior for clues about how, as Christians, they are to behave in certain situations. If they hear us use profanity, they feel that gives them permission to use profanity. If they see us using alcohol, they assume that this gives them permission to use alcohol. There may be some cases in which we will want to sacrifice our own rights to do some of these kinds of things because we are aware of how serious and literal the message is they give to our students.

Does that mean that we are disqualified from nurturing students because we are not yet perfect? Certainly not. Modeling the Christian life is allowing students to watch us seek to live out a life in fellowship with Jesus. In fact, one of the most important aspects of our modeling of the Christian life might be allowing our students to observe how we deal with disobedience and guilt in our own lives. They can learn from our failures as well as our successes.

There are some ways that we can guard ourselves as models to make sure that we are neither cloning our students nor misleading them. In *A Practical Theology of Spirituality* (Zondervan, 1987) Larry Richards offers these four guidelines: (a) We must be totally committed to the authority of Scripture as a guide for faith and practice; (b) We must be committed to Christ's lordship in our own lives and open to hearing and obeying his word; (c) We must be accountable to one another in the body of Christ, that our insights might be shaped and tested by other believers; and (d) We need to listen to the historic voice of the church. That keeps us from taking "our" disciples on a tangent away from being Jesus' disciples.

FROM MENTOR
TO PEER

As students move into the later years of high school, we will want to encourage them to depend less on us and more on Jesus as their model. There comes a point when an adolescent Elisha has to follow the Lord on his own without the presence or model of an adult Elijah. That shift is reflected in Paul's ministry.

If we read his letter to a less mature church, such as the church in Corinth, we hear him saying, "Follow my example, as I follow the example of Christ" (1 Corinthians 11:1). But as he addresses the more spiritually mature believers in Ephesus, notice that he writes, "Be imitators of God" (Ephesians 5:1). There is a weaning process there that suggests we will come to a point when we will want to encourage students not to say, "What would Duffy do?" or "What would Sherry do?" but "What would Jesus do?"

When we read Paul's encouragement to the strong church in Thessalonica, we can even see how the cycle of modeling begins again as we nurture students into deeper maturity. "You know how we lived among you for your sake. *You became imitators of us and of the Lord*; in spite of severe suffering, you welcomed the message with the joy given by the Holy Spirit. *And so you became a model* to all the believers in Macedonia and Achaia" (1 Thessalonians 1:5–7).

Perhaps one of the ways we can best utilize this material is by stopping to consider the challenge of modeling the Christian life. As an individual or as a ministry team, we might strengthen our ministry of nurture by carefully thinking through and dealing with these questions:

- If my students were exactly like me, how would they be most like Jesus?
- If my students were exactly like me, how would they be least like Jesus?
- What am I teaching my students about a Christian lifestyle by my model?

3. *Help Them to Establish and Deepen Their Commitment to God*

As we begin to nurture in students a deeper and deeper commitment to Christ, we are calling students to be disciples of Jesus Christ. A disciple is, technically, a learner, a student. In terms of spiritual growth, I think of teenagers as disciples when they have decided to take the initiative for their own spiritual growth. They have decided, in effect, to *discipline* themselves for growth, even if the rest of their friends, and the larger group, is not as motivated to move forward.

Our mandate is to call students to this kind of discipleship. It is especially important that we encourage students to grow deeper at this point because there seems to be a special opportunity with the new believer that we lose after they have been in the faith for awhile. Most of us in youth ministry have seen students blast off like rockets after their initial commitment and then slow into more of a business-as-usual orbit pattern at a later point. If we say, "We're going to wait until they're older" or "We're going to go slowly because we don't want to push them too fast," we may face losing excellent opportunities to help them grow.

For one thing new believers are vulnerable. We can't afford to become lax in our responsibility or they may feel that their commitment was just a bleep on the radar — just an emotional experience.

Secondly, new Christians seem to be the ones who are most susceptible to change. When Katie started bringing Jim to youth group, he was open but non-committal. It was obvious that he was thinking this whole proposition through very carefully. But when he did finally make a commitment, I found a teachability in him that I didn't sense in a lot of the more mature Christian kids in the group. He was ready to reconsider everything about his whole life. It was as if the time was ripe. I worried that things were moving so fast, but I also sensed that God was doing something unique in this guy, and we should not let the opportunity pass.

In the words of the Apostle Paul, "So then, just as you received Christ Jesus as Lord, continue to live in him, rooted and built up in him, strengthened in the faith as you were taught, and overflowing with thankfulness. See to it that no one takes you captive through hollow and deceptive philosophy, which depends on human tradition and the basic principles of this world rather than on Christ" (Colossians 2:6-8).

"CONTINUE TO LIVE IN HIM"

At the core of the Christian life is commitment—obedience to Christ. Jesus told his followers in John 13:15, "I have set you an example that you should do as I have done for you." We cannot nurture students without working through the nitty-gritty issues of how they live their lives in obedience to God. As we begin to help students establish and deepen their commitment, we must add to the relational ministry a strong ministry of teaching and accountability.

In *Essentials of Discipleship* (NavPress, 1980), Fran Cosgrove reminds us that perfect obedience doesn't happen overnight. As we've observed earlier in the book, growth and maturity take time. Cosgrove notes that there are five stages of obedience that we move through in the Christian life.

Stage one is essentially disobedience. It says in effect, "I am going to do what I want to do regardless of what God wants me to do." The second stage of obedience shows some shift in a more positive direction. It is best represented by the phrase, "If God will give me what I want first, then I will give him an equal exchange." At stage three the attitude is a bit more open: "If God will give me what I want first, then I will give him what he wants."

By stage four we see signs of genuine commitment: "I will give God what he wants first, then in faith I believe that he will give me what I want." Stage five represents full and open obedience to God: "I will give God whatever he wants regardless of whether he gives me what I want."

This five-stage scheme reminds us that teenagers can be making progress in the journey of obedience even if they have not yet reached the destination. Jesus never watered down his emphasis on the importance of absolute obedience to God. He never tried to soften the edge of that message to make it more appealing to his audience. That's a mistake we often make.

In Luke 9:57–62, Luke recounts an interesting series of statements made by Jesus:

> As they were walking along the road, a man said to him, "I will follow you wherever you go." Jesus replied, "Foxes have holes and birds of the air have nests, but the Son of man has no place to lay his head." He said to another man, "Follow me." But the man replied, "Lord, first let me go and bury my father." Jesus said to him, "Let the dead bury their own dead, but you go and proclaim the kingdom of God." Still another said, "I will follow you Lord; but first let me go back and say good-bye to my family." Jesus replied, "No one who puts his hand to the plow and looks back is fit for service in the Kingdom of God" (Luke 9:57–62).

It is important for us to note as youth ministers is that Jesus challenged each of these people to full obedience. He didn't sacrifice that challenge for the sake of adding followers. It doesn't take any church growth expert to note that in this one short passage, Jesus just turned away three prospective members.

The other lesson we need to note in this passage is that even though Jesus said, "No one who puts his hand to the plow and looks back is fit for service in the Kingdom of God," he clearly was willing to work with and nurture people like Peter (and the other disciples) who often made precisely that kind of backward look.

Recently I sat in my office talking with a young woman who was struggling with obedience in her relationship with her boyfriend. She was fearful that if she refused his sexual advances, he would leave her. Through her tears she finally came to the point where she decided to leave this guy, but it was clear that she was holding God responsible for doing his part and finding her another boyfriend.

Now obviously that is not a picture of complete obedience, of abandonment to the will of God and of walking by faith. But it *is* a step in the right direction. I'm convinced that sometimes our students get discouraged because they are partially obedient and we seem to be displeased unless they move for total obedience. We are fearful that if we affirm them for anything less than total obedience we are giving them the wrong message. There may some truth to that. But we also need to realize that obedience is usually marked off in baby steps— not giant steps. J.L. Williams put it this way: "God is easy to please, but hard to satisfy."

A ministry of establishing and building starts from the ground up. We begin with students where they are and grow them from there. Each student's pilgrimage will be unique. Our job is not to start with them where we are, or where we want them to be. Our calling is to start with them where they are and move them forward into maturity from that point.

THE IMPORTANCE OF
A CHURCH FELLOWSHIP

One of the best ways to nurture Christian obedience in teenage disciples is to help them to become intimately involved with a local church fellowship. So many times our Christian teenagers assume that if they are active in one-on-one discipleship, that is enough. It is not. It is discouraging how many serious Christian college students go away to school and the very first habit that they decide to leave at home is involvement in a local church. Sunday morning comes and the dorm is filled with students who have chosen to worship at The

First Church of the Sleeping Saints. One of the significant findings of Merton Strommen's well-known study, *The Five Cries of Youth* (New York: Harper & Row, 1974) is that attending and being active in the life of a local church is one of the best indicators of the probable longevity of a teenager's walk with Christ.

How can a local church, with all of its problems, "boring" worship services, and politics, be this significant? First of all, it offers protection. In Hebrews 3:12 and 13, the writer reminds us of the importance of a fellowship in helping us to see beyond our blindspots of disobedience: "See to it, brothers, that none of you has a sinful, unbelieving heart that turns away from the living God. But encourage one another daily, as long as it is called Today, so that none of you may be hardened by sin's deceitfulness."

Secondly, students need a fellowship of believers to offer them encouragement and stimulation (Hebrews 10:24, 25). This is especially critical for teenage believers. Third, a fellowship offers students a context in which they can share and confess their needs to other believers, and pray for one another (Acts 2:42). Paul writes, "Brothers, if someone is caught in a sin, you who are spiritual should restore him gently. But watch yourself, or you also may be tempted. Carry each other's burdens, and in this way you will fulfill the law of Christ" (Galatians 6:1, 2). I have found this simple principle to be one of the absolute keys for encouraging students in their obedience to Jesus.

Finally, teenagers need to be taught the value of corporate worship. When all the old youth-group strategies have come and gone, when we have exhausted all the bells and whistles, it will be the meaningful worship experiences which allow students to genuinely experience the presence of God (Colossians 3:16).

One youth minister held a Stupid Night with her group—a night when everything the entire evening is done backwards. The evening begins with the closing statement: "We hope everybody had a great time, and thanks for coming." And then it goes on from there. Movies are shown backwards. Clothes are worn backwards. Games are played backwards. *Everything* is backwards.

She concluded the evening with a Stupid Worship Service, which, of course, is what most kids think a worship service is anyway. It was very simple. It consisted of a service of communion during which the youth minister read through the last statements Jesus made from the cross. And each time she read a statement, the students responded in a liturgy with the statement, "That's stupid."

She worked her way through the statements: "Here is your mother" (John 19:27); "I am thirsty" (John 19:28); "It is finished" (John 19:30), and each time the students responded with, "That's stupid." Finally she got to those words, "Father forgive them, for they do not know what they are doing" (Luke 23:34). The room got very quiet and the mood was sober. And she closed with Paul's words in 1 Corinthians 1:18, 25—"For the message of the cross is foolishness to those who are perishing, but to us who are being saved it is the power of God . . . For the foolishness of God is wiser than man's wisdom, and the weakness of God is stronger than man's strength."

With the room full of students standing around with their clothes on backwards, it was a very powerful experience.

And it didn't happen with a game or a Bible study or even with a one-on-one meeting. It happened through a liturgy of worship.

A PRACTICAL SUGGESTION

Because there are so many different areas in which we need to help students monitor their obedience to Christ, one of the biggest problems is simply being able to keep track of all the different students and all of their different needs for growth. One helpful idea helpful was conceived by Mike Rowe, former Youth Minister at Trinity Baptist Church in Nashua, New Hampshire.

Faced with a youth group that was quickly growing in number, he wanted to come up with some means by which he could continue to track the individual growth of each student. To help in this regard he developed the following chart for each student in his group:

Student's Name: _____ Phone: _____

Birthday: _____ Yr. of Graduation: ____

AREA OF GROWTH

WALK WITH GOD:

Devotional Life:

Loves God above all else . . . .☐
Has a consistent quiet time . . . .☐
Is learning and applying God's Word. . . . .☐
Memorizes and meditates on Scripture. . . . .☐
Understands/practices personal worship . . . .☐
Has a consistent personal prayer life . . . .☐

Doctrine:

Has a working knowledge of following:
Scripture . . . .☐
God the Father . . . .☐
Jesus Christ . . . .☐
Holy Spirit . . . .☐
Man, Sin, and Salvation . . . .☐
Assurance of Salvation. . . . .☐
Church and Sacraments. . . . .☐

Daily Life:

Is developing a positive self-image based
on Scripture . . . .☐
Life is motivated by a biblical understanding
of justification (not by guilt). . . . .☐
Demonstrates a lifestyle of submission to God
and his Word (i.e. Lordship) . . . .☐
Makes goals and sets priorities . . . .☐
Manages time well . . . .☐

FELLOWSHIP:

Body Life:

Has a love for God's people . . . .☐
Understands biblical fellowship . . . .☐
Uses the tongue to build up the body . . . .☐
Demonstrates compassion and servanthood. . . . .☐
Knows and uses Spiritual gifts. . . . .☐
Is committed to a local church . . . .☐

Understands and practices biblical giving . . . .☐

Making Disciples:
Is able to follow-up a new believer . . . .☐
Has discipled, or is discipling a younger believer . . . .☐
Is able to explain the Gospel to another person. . . . . .☐

EVANGELISM:
Is motivated by a love for God, a concern for
the lost and a zeal for God's glory . . . .☐
Is actively seeking to share the Gospel . . . .☐
Has been taught how to share the Gospel . . . .☐
Has shared the Gospel with someone. . . . .☐
Can share a three to five minute personal testimony. .☐
Has shared his or her testimony with a friend
or group. . . . .☐
Has a working knowledge of basic apologetics . . . . . .☐

The problem of course, is that as soon as someone mentions a system like this, people can find all kinds of reasons not to like it: too mechanical, too cut-and-dried, too simplistic; it leaves out some important areas. And no doubt, some of these criticisms are valid. It should be noted that we have not provided here the entire list that Mike and his leaders use. And to some extent, what is included in the list is going to vary with each ministry and each youth minister anyway.

What this youth minister tried to do, and what all of us must struggle with, is to assume some personal responsibility for the kids in the youth groups. As shepherds we need to ask, "How can I track these students in my group so that this ministry does not become so impersonal that I lose sight of how students are making progress in learning how to obey God?" If this strategy can help some youth workers tighten up their ministry, it is worth looking at.

TEENAGERS WILL STILL BE TEENAGERS

Maybe the most important point for us to remember in calling students to discipleship is that high-school students are still going to act like high-school students. How many of us have had the experience of sharing a powerful time of commitment with a group of students on a retreat, and then on the way home in the van, those same spiritually vibrant students, who only hours earlier were weeping and praying before God, are now in the back of the van burping, joking around, and generally acting like bozos? But that is the nature of a teenage disciple.

Just because students get serious about a relationship with Jesus doesn't mean they are suddenly going to start acting like adults (praise the Lord!), wearing leisure suits, and listening to tapes by George Beverly Shea.

INFANT MORTALITY

One of the tragedies of life in modern-day America is the growing rate of infant mortality. How sad that a new life, with all of the promise and the hope that it brings, should be so soon ended due to inadequate care or neglect.

Equally tragic is the number of new Christians who are born again by the Spirit of God and then are never adequately followed up with nurture and care. Each year youth ministries across this country spend countless hours, dollars, and resources trying to reach out and touch teenagers for Jesus Christ. How sad it is that after going to all of the human and monetary expense of touching these students, we often let them slip from our grasp. My prayer with this chapter is that we would go beyond bringing newborn Christians home to our church families, and that we would assume the ongoing and time-consuming task of parenting and nurturing. If we will recommit ourselves to this priority we can help these young people learn to stand, then learn to walk. We can help them mature to the point that, like Elijah, we can release and commission them to reproduce themselves spiritually in the lives of others. That is the fourth and final phase of the Master's Plan.

CHAPTER FIFTEEN
EQUIPPING FOR MINISTRY

The major imperative in youth work is to help youth into a sense of mission, of being sent for a purpose and a task. It is to know the sense of purposefulness that grips the person who has responded to God's love.

Dr. Merton Strommen,
Five Cries of Youth

CALL THEM TO SERVICE

Francis Xavier, the Jesuit director of missions in India, China, and Japan in the sixteenth century, once said that he longed to be back in his native Paris, "to go shouting up and down the streets, to tell the students to give up their small ambitions and come eastward and to preach the Gospel of Jesus Christ." The final stage of the Master's Plan for nurture and discipleship was calling his disciples to a life of service, entrusting to them the ministry of the kingdom. In the same way, we have not completed our task of nurture until we have challenged and equipped our students to give up their small ambitions for the sake of the Gospel. This is the fourth and final critical phase of the Master's Plan.

A MENTALITY OF SERVANTHOOD

Something happened in the late sixties and early seventies in America. One nationwide survey of church youth at that time showed heightened interest in social issues like the Viet Nam War, a mandatory draft, world peace, an unresponsive government, social injustices, and the huge chasm between ideals and realities in every-day life.

People began to talk about issues bigger than themselves. Students burned draft cards. Protests and riots erupted on college campuses, and a movie starlet named Jane Fonda (fresh from her consciousness-raising screen role in *Barbarella*) protested the Vietnam War by making a "good-will" trip to North Vietnam. A young radical named Abbie Hoffman wrote *Steal This Book*, and a young California folk singer wrote the song, "Eve of Destruction."

But something shifted in the late seventies and the eighties. What researcher Merton Strommen had once called the "cry of social protest" among America's youth diminished to a faint whimper. Jane Fonda began selling thirty-dollar videos to help yuppies stay in good physical shape. The voices of the leading radicals were, in some cases, muffled by drug overdoses or drowned out by the ticker tape of a Wall Street brokerage house. Their protesting days were over. The tie-dyed shirts gave way to business suits. And Barry McGuire, the young, gravel-voiced protest singer, became a Christian and eventually moved to New Zealand.

What emerged in the eighties is described by Jay Kesler, President of Taylor University, as a generation of teenagers marked by "profound apathy." We find ourselves faced with teenagers who make up what Eastern College Sociology professor Tony Campolo describes as a "passionless generation." Research confirms that he is right:

- Researchers from the National Center for Educational Statistics asked collegians fifteen years ago, "How concerned are you about correcting social and economic inequalities?" In 1972 twenty-seven percent of the students responded "very concerned." By 1980 only thirteen percent responded in the same way.

- Over the past fifteen years an ever-increasing number of college freshman stated that "being well-off financially" was an important goal for them. A record high seventy-three percent of students surveyed responded that way in 1987. Meanwhile, over the same period the importance of "developing a meaningful philosophy of life" has been steadily diminishing, a major concern of only forty-three percent of college students surveyed in 1987.

- A Gallup poll showed that between March 1981 and October 1985, participation in volunteer services dropped from fifty-four percent to forty-three percent among eighteen-to-twenty-four-year-olds.

"THE TIMES
THEY ARE A'CHANGIN' "

As people who are concerned about teenagers, we cannot help but observe these shifts and ask, "Why?" What has happened that has bred a generation of teenagers with small ambitions? Maybe nothing. Jonathan Yardley, in an excellent commentary for the Washington Post, suggests that the sixties were every bit as selfish as the seventies and eighties. It was just that then the best parties, the cheapest drugs, and the loosest women happened to be a part of the protest movement. As an alumnus of that generation, I think Yardley is probably correct.

Some commentators see deeper reasons, a compromise of dreams — a generation of teenagers who basically changed the questions so that the answers would fit better.

Others suggest that the permissiveness that grew out of the sixties had a numbing effect on teenagers. Why should they care about sweeping social changes during an era of personal permissiveness? If they can get what they want, why should they take to the streets? Vance Packard's *The Sexual Wilderness* (McKay Co., 1968) lends support to this notion by stating that there is significant evidence of an inverse correlation between increase in sexual permissiveness and the amount of college campus activism.

Or perhaps the reason we see this shift is that, as Wilmington, North Carolina psychologist Bruce A. Baldwin puts it, we have raised a generation of "cornucopia kids," children who are "over-indulged and pampered by their competitive, guilt-ridden, yuppie parents" (*Beyond the Cornucopia Kids: How To Raise Healthy, Achieving Children*, (Direction Dynamics, 1988). Baldwin sees the horn of plenty image as being the perfect illustration of today's problem of too much too soon.

"This is an epidemic afflicting as many as one out of every five children in this country," according to Baldwin. "Children with cornucopia complexes grow up expecting that the good life will always be available for the asking, without effort or need for personal accountability."

A veteran of eighteen years of children's practice, Baldwin goes on to identify characteristics of the cornucopia complex:

- Children expect to get what they want whenever they want it, and only the top of the line;
- They often throw tantrums to get their way;
- They have difficulty entertaining themselves and they become easily bored;
- They do not expect to face consequences for their actions.

People who spend much time with teenagers will recognize some of these very traits in the average youth group.

Then there are those who take what is described as the *phenomenological* approach to the question. Those of this school of thought believe that the best way to understand the student apathy of today is not by looking to their past, but by looking to their future. One such reason teenagers aren't that excited about life might be that there really isn't that much to get excited about. There is nothing to challenge them, no calling that awakens their sense of heroism.

Perhaps the most reasonable answer can be traced back to the way we have elevated selfishness in our culture. The modern credo is no longer "Ask not what your country can do for you, but what you can do for your country." The modern credo is "Do something nice for yourself." Billy Joel espouses this kind of individualism when he sings, "I don't care what you say anymore, this is my life! Go ahead with your own life; leave me alone." This kind of selfishness breeds service only when serving feels good—the Live-Aid mentality that says, "Let's raise money for the hungry by going to an all-day rock 'n' roll concert where we can do drugs and dig the vibes."

Even the Christian community has discovered that selfishness is more easily marketed than service. One church in California offers a money-back guarantee to parishioners who give a tithe to the church if they do not feel that God has returned their gift to them many times over.

Whether or not any or all of these diagnosticians are right is hard to say. Probably they all have hit on some part of the truth. Regardless of our thoughts, those of us in youth ministry cannot deny that developing a mentality of service is probably the most difficult building block in the ministry of nurture.

We are working with students who do not feel they can make much of a contribution. Their low self-esteem prompts them to try little because they suspect that they will fail. Often we in youth ministry play right into the hands of that mindset by expecting very little, because we are afraid high expectations may alienate someone from the group. In short, too many youth ministries typically cater to small ambitions.

In stark contrast to a mentality that tells us to get all we can, Jesus called his disciples to a lifestyle of service. We read about this in John 13:12–17:

> When (Jesus) had finished washing their feet, he put on his clothes and returned to his place. "Do you understand what I have done for you?" he asked them. "You call me 'Teacher' and 'Lord,' and rightly so, for that is what I am. Now that I, your Lord and Teacher, have washed your feet, you also should wash one another's feet. I have set you an example that you should do as I have done for you. I tell you the truth, no servant is greater than his master, nor is a messenger greater than the one who sent him. Now that you know these things, you will be blessed if you do them."

HOW DO WE BUILD A MENTALITY OF SERVICE?

Most youth ministers agree that fostering an attitude of service is an important part of nurture. The question is, how can we motivate students to care? Essentially, there are three approaches:

- **Guilt,** or negative pressure ("There are hungry children starving all over the globe tonight and all you can think about is going downstairs for pizza after youth meeting?")

- **Goad,** or positive pressure ("Come on, guys, if we don't do something about this now, we never will.")
- **Guide,** or exposing students to situations in which God can move them and mold their hearts ("I'm going to take a van load of folks into the city next Monday night to work at the Rescue Center. I would like to have some of you go down with me.")

GUIDING STUDENTS INTO SERVICE

In *Ways to Help Them Learn—Youth* (Gospel Light, 1971), David A. Stoop has written that the learning process usually takes us through four stages. The first is *familiarization*. If we desire to guide our students into a life of service we must use some strategies that will give them familiarity with the need and the call. The Compassion Project (prepared by Rich Van Pelt and Jim Hancock), from Compassion International (P.O. Box 7000, Colorado Springs, Colorado 80933-7000) is an example of the kind of tool that we can use to give students some familiarity with the whole mentality of service. Utilizing simulation games, music, Bible studies, and discussion starters, the creators of this project offer youth workers several different avenues to approach servanthood.

Stoop's next step is *feedback*. For the learning process to be effective, students must have a chance to discuss and offer feedback about the input they've received. Ridge Burns, who heads up the Center for Student Missions in California, has often remarked that when he takes students into downtown Los Angeles for the first time and they see some of the poorest of the poor, or when he takes students into the hospital to the AIDS ward, students need to talk about what they've seen. They need to be given a chance to reflect on their feelings and their thoughts. If we just show students the bloated babies, and give them the horror stories without allowing them an opportunity for feedback, it can become for them something almost detached from reality—like a scary movie that one watches and then easily forgets.

Exploration is the third phase of learning. At this point, we want to give students a chance to explore various ways that they can serve.

We want to allow them to try out various kinds of service. Some students are going to stretch their spiritual muscles through a ministry within the youth program. Others may want to try their hand in a service project away from church property. The key here is that the youth minister needs to get students out there and expose them to various kinds of service.

Mike Yaconelli, who along with his wife, Karla, heads up a Young Life club in Yreka, California, every Easter takes a group of students to do a work project in Tijuana, Mexico. He tells the story about the first trip he put together, and how he had sought to involve other youth groups from his area. One group had apparently signed on for the trip, and then about one week before the day of departure, the group backed out. In asking why the group had decided to back out at the last minute, the youth minister told Mike, "Not that many of my kids are sure they want to do it."

Of course, the reality of the situation was that not many of the kids from Yreka Young Life were sure they wanted to do it, either. But that was precisely the point. The kids need a chance to explore the idea, and they don't get that chance sitting at home. Mike took his group to Tijuana that first year, a small group of students who had no idea what they were getting into. Over the course of that week, they built several houses, had an incredible time, and finished up their week with a candlelight service and a time of testimony. The students came back home to Yreka totally excited.

The following Easter, when it was time to go to Mexico again, it was all Mike could do to make room for everyone that wanted to go. There was excitement. There was momentum. And it was because he had given his group a chance for exploration—an opportunity to discover that they wanted to serve and were capable of serving.

According to Stoop, the last stage of the learning process is *responsibility*. As our youth move into later years of high school and into college, we are then going to want to emphasize not just the possibility of service—but the responsibility for service. We are going to want to challenge students to move out in answer to the call of God.

That does not mean that every student will need to go to the mission field or that they will need to head into the ministry. But we do need to help students understand that God is interested in their vocation. Each year the Pittsburgh Coalition for Christian Outreach sponsors the Jubilee Conference in which college students hear from lawyers, doctors, scientists, teachers, and professionals from all walks of life who are utilizing their professional work as a ministry. It is a good way of helping students to come to grips with their responsibility to serve.

To state it in a shorter form, if we want to nurture a mentality of servanthood in our students, our youth program will need to provide *information* about needs to be met, *examples* of the ways that students can meet these needs, and *opportunities* to go out and try meeting these needs.

The one essential in this whole process is what Robert Crandall describes in his essay "Youth Serving the Church" as matching the appropriate challenge with the appropriate age group (*Youth Education in the Church*, ed. Zuck and Benson, Moody Press, 1978). In developing a servant's heart, we are going to use different approaches at different stages of the students' growth and spiritual maturity. For example, our approach might be best broken down this way:

- **Junior high.** Emphasis on "You *should* be involved in service." This consists mostly of familiarization and feedback.
- **Senior high.** Emphasis on "You *could* be serving." A major part of our strategy here is in actual exploration.
- **Post-high school/college.** Emphasis on "*Would you be willing?*" We are talking at this point about assuming some specific responsibility for ministry in some capacity.

TWO KINDS OF SERVICE

In youth ministry today there are at least two distinct ways that we think of service. One is in terms of personally equipping kids to do ministry among their peers—the ministry of multiplication that so characterized the work of Jesus and Paul. The second is in terms of reaching out to those in need—in short, developing a mentality of servanthood. This is a type of service that might be fleshed out in mission projects and service activities. As we examine this last element of the Master's Plan, we want to consider both.

PERSONAL MINISTRY—
MINISTRY ON THE INSIDE

Teenagers are the people best equipped to do ministry with teenagers. To be sure, they need adult guidance, they need adult training, and they need adult supervision. But teenagers can be equipped to do significant ministry within a youth program. That is the first key point we need to affirm. Well-trained teenagers can serve at all levels of a ministry.

If we study the ministry of Jesus in the gospels, we note that the first year his disciples were with him, they did very little. Their ministry was basically one of support and learning. But shortly after that first year, Jesus seemed to be ready to send them out on their own. Using that same pattern, we can utilize students for personal ministry within our youth programs. What kinds of tasks they do will vary from program to program, but our challenge is to discern their gifts, develop those gifts, and deploy those gifts.

David Stoop suggests that this process of training and deployment breaks down into four key phases. He refers to them as the "four phases of ease":

- I do it—you watch
- We do it together
- You do it—I watch
- You do it—I go train someone else

This kind of training can be instituted in a number of different ways, but the sequence is important. For example, in helping train some of my youth-group students in how to do Bible study, I might begin by just saying, "Look, you've been watching me do Bible study for a long time now. Why don't you help me? Four weeks from tonight I am going to be doing a Bible study in Nehemiah. I'm going to give you the material now so that you can look it over. What I suggest is that I will do the first section of the Bible study, you do the second and third sections, and I will do the fourth section. We will do the study together."

In time, as the student is comfortable with doing a portion of the study along with me, I might then encourage him to try doing it alone some week while I watch. Then, I can critique, encourage, and help him to fine tune his skills.

Finally, the student is ready to do the Bible study on his own, without my partnership and without me present. At that point, I can focus my training on someone else. The student can begin to work with someone else he wants to train, and the ministry is multiplied by a factor of two.

That kind of hand-off is one of the scariest and most exciting parts of ministry. And yet it is at the heart of equipping students for service. In one church where I served, we actually developed one whole program largely so that students who were ready would have an arena in which to stretch and exercise their spiritual gifts could do so. It was a small group ministry that involved about eight individual students working with eight different groups of five kids each.

We met with these students once a month to train them in small group technique. We discussed how to set the right environment. We talked about different kinds of questions that can be used in a small group. We talked about some of the Groupbusters that can make a group hard to lead. In short, it was a small youth workers' institute for students in the youth group.

What we found was that these students began to take on more and more ministry ownership. They began visiting the students in their groups. They did service projects with their small groups. They even planned their own small group lock-ins (Boy, were we psyched about that!). What we had, in effect, was several small ministries or "house churches" within our larger youth program, and a growing number of teenagers who were basically youth leaders for their small five-person groups.

This leadership role should be taken seriously. For students to serve in this capacity they will need to be trained in six key areas: 1) they will need to be effective in basic evangelism; 2) they will need to demonstrate some consistency in their own spiritual walk; 3) they will need to be able to motivate others; 4) they will need to be trained to do follow-up; 5) they will need to be trained how to train others like themselves; and 6) they will need to be self-starters.

We don't need to wait until a student is proficient in all areas before we use them in a few areas. Probably, it is wisest to give students initially some kind of physical responsibility—e.g., "Would you please be here early to set up the chairs?" or "Could you help us with the tape loan library?"

Then as students demonstrate more responsibility, we are able to give them personal responsibilities—e.g., "We had a new student visit tonight for the first time. Would you give him a call this week and let him know we were glad to see him here?" Again, as students prove faithful at that level of responsibility, we can then give them deeper personal responsibilities: i.e., "Would you be willing to lead a small Grow Group this fall?"

It is quite possible that we will not get to see all of these qualities built into the students by the time they leave our nurture. That is not failure. Our task is simply to be consistent in equipping them and moving them forward.

MISSIONS AND SERVICE— MINISTRY ON THE OUTSIDE

There are four basic kinds of service projects in which we can involve teenagers. Let's look at each type of project.

1. *Information: Raise Awareness*

The main goal at this stage is simply to provide information. Especially with younger teens, our most appropriate goal would be to raise their awareness of the need and the call to serve God in the world.

2. *Observation: Raise Eyebrows*

The difference between this kind of project and the Information project is that with an Observation project students gain information firsthand. For example, one of the projects that several youth ministers have undertaken is Urban Plunge, where students will go into an inner-city setting for a weekend and be allowed to observe for themselves the sights, sounds, and smells of the city. Perhaps they will sleep in an inner-city church, or work in a soup kitchen, but the idea is to give students a chance to make their own observations.

Some denominational programs give students an opportunity for this kind of observation on an international level. One United Methodist youth worker in Florida took her youth group to Haiti to see the kinds of work done by the United Methodist Church in Haiti. Obviously, the major thrust of this kind of project is going to be familiarization. If a youth worker does not make wise use of feedback and follow-up this kind of trip carefully, it will bear no more lasting fruit than a summer vacation.

Obviously, when a youth worker is thinking about a project at this level, there are certain questions that bear asking:

- Wouldn't money spent on a mission trip be better spent if we just sent the money? Can we justify going just to observe?
- Trips to Haiti are becoming so popular; what are we really accomplishing?
- Are kids coming for the right reason, or do they just want to get out of the house? Is there a kind of upper-class voyeurism at work here—the upper-class, suburban kids coming into the city to see how the lower class lives?
- What good is it to give the kids this kind of emphasis when the money might be better used by giving this kind of experience to adults in the church?

None of these questions necessarily precludes an observation project, but they are worth thinking about in advance.

3. *Participation: Raise a Building*
This kind of service project actually has to do with any kind of hands-on labor. This might involve building church pews, painting a building, cleaning up a deserted yard, building a playground, or building a house. This may be a project across town or across the border, or even down the street from the church. (For a complete look at foreign mission trips and work projects, see Paul Borthwick's *Youth*

and Missions, Victor Books, 1988. For additional information about other kinds of service projects, see Tony Campolo's *Ideas for Social Action*, Youth Specialties/Zondervan, 1985.)

Some of the ideas that can be used for this kind of project:

Service Scavenger Hunt—Prepare a list of service activities that students can do as part of a scavenger hunt. The list might read, "Clean ten windows; wash one car; raise ten dollars for Compassion International; pick up one garbage bag of trash; visit one shut-in," etc. Students work in teams to complete the list of items in the scavenger hunt.

Smoke Alarm Ministry—The irony of smoke alarms is that the elderly, who need them the most because it takes them the longest to get out of the house, are the least able to install the alarms. The idea here is that students in your youth group install smoke alarms for elderly people in your community who cannot or will not climb up on a ladder to install one. Sometimes fire departments are even willing to give the smoke alarms to the youth group if the youth group will install them. The end result is a tangible, life-saving ministry.

Halloween Party for Neighborhood Children—In an effort to do some kind of community outreach, our youth group started hosting an annual Halloween Party for all the children in town. We utilized the church basement and set up a haunted house in one section of hallways, and a game room in the fellowship hall. Different kids ran the ring toss, go-fish, and others. Area merchants provided prizes and food. The highlight of the affair was the wheelbarrow ride around the church building. We put some hay in some wheelbarrows and gave the children indoor hay rides. The project provided a safe, fun Halloween with supervision for the children, and it definitely made us some friends around the community.

Year-Round Christmas Caroling—Almost every youth group makes some sort of annual pilgrimage to the local rest home to sing carols at Christmas. That's fine. But what might actually be more appreciated is a once-a-month or once-a-quarter trip to the rest home. The difference would be that instead of singing Christmas carols, the group could sing some of the old hymns that residents want to hear.

A Youth Group Shower—Each month Calvary Church (Charlotte, North Carolina) youth minister Tim Tinsley leads his senior highs in a help project, which has included mending fences, cleaning basements, raking leaves, etc. The group is committed to finding needs and then doing whatever it takes to fill them.

In thinking about his group's next project Tim was put in touch with the Charlotte (NC) Area Fund. A representative from the organization was invited to come out and talk to the youth group about someone they could help. The youth group learned about Lisa, a 17-year-old mother of a little boy. When Lisa was eleven, her stepfather began regularly abusing her sexually. She was soon pregnant with Cal, who was now three. Lisa also had a little girl, Elizabeth, just eighteen months old. Lisa loved her children and wanted the best for them, but early motherhood and adult responsibilities cut short her own childhood.

The youth group at Calvary Church decided to host a giant baby shower for Lisa so she could get some things that would help her young family. Gifts included a refrigerator, carpet, plates, a space heater, drapes, various pieces of furniture, a substantial food supply, and money for paying overdue bills. It was a wonderful way of allowing students to get involved in service.

Despite the fact that any of these projects could have a very positive impact on a youth group, we should be aware that any youth minister who tries to move his group in this direction is going to face some questions. These are the issues that are generally raised in connection with this kind of project:

- Do we ever have the right/responsibility to suggest political action to our youth groups?
- What if we start the project and kids don't sustain their interest?
- Are we ready for the parent who is going to say, "Sure the kids will clean a field in Appalachia, but they won't clean up their rooms! Why don't you tell them to do that?"

4. *Donations: Raise Funds*

The thrust of this sort of mission project is clear and simple: a youth ministry is seeking to raise funds for some sort of missions project. While this effort is praiseworthy and noble, it has some significant drawbacks. One is that some students would love to throw money at certain problems so that they can avoid nitty-gritty, down-to-earth involvement. Second, by putting the students at the fund-raising end of the equation instead of at the giving end of the equation, we really steal from them the chance to meet the people who will most benefit by it. That's unfortunate because the satisfaction of the giver is lowered significantly.

When youth ministers decide to use a donation project, it is absolutely imperative that they adhere to strict policies of money-handling and reporting. Here are some suggestions:

- Be sure the youth group understands how the money will be used. The more specific, the better.
- Consider maintaining support over long period of time. A long-term donation is a better way of building your group's emotional investment in a project. With a one-time gift, the attention shifts quickly to some other project or activity.
- Allow young people to give their own money. Discourage them from going home and talking their parents into making a donation. In terms of learning value, the project that earns a little money, all from the students, is far better than the one which earns a lot of money, most of it from two or three wealthy adult contributors.
- Limit fund-raising to worthy projects. It is worth asking whether or not a youth group is justified in raising money for a ski trip or youth-group activity. My suggestion is not to do it. When you do need to raise that money for a mission trip, you do not want the people in the church wondering how the money will end up being used.
- Set a goal. People work better and harder when they are working toward a goal.
- Beware of too much of the same strategy. Beware "A-thon-athons."

DISCOVERING THE JOY OF SERVICE

No matter what a youth minister tries to do, service and giving are the kinds of ideas that simply cannot be learned well without hands-on, active involvement. On the other hand, one of the most exciting aspects of utilizing students in some form of ministry or service is that students who are involved get very excited about God using them. There is a part of that excitement and vision that only God can put inside a person. To that extent, Christ's instruction is that we pray to the Lord of the harvest for workers. But we can give students opportunities, training, and encouragement to "give up their small ambitions."

SECTION
FOUR

CONCLUSION

CHAPTER SIXTEEN

A CHALLENGE, SOME GOOD ADVICE, AND A BUILDING CODE

A CHALLENGE

There is a television commercial that probably provides for us the best challenge for closing this book. The ad sells tennis shoes with the simple exhortation, "Just do it." Any person reading this book could probably think of a hundred reasons why they cannot or do not wish to build the kind of ministry that genuinely nurtures spiritual growth in teenagers. We're afraid of failure. We're afraid of teenagers. We don't feel adequate. We aren't cool. The list goes on and on.

Our claim to victory as we embark on this adventure of ministry is not staked in our own gifts or our own strategies and resources. It is staked on the bedrock fact that we do not go out alone. Paul reminds us in 1 Thessalonians 5:24, "The one who calls you is faithful and he will do it." With all due respect to the tennis shoe people, that's really where the rubber meets the road. We can do this ministry, not because we decide to just do it, but because God will do it through us.

SOME GOOD ADVICE

Each year, along with a team of about six others, I travel to about fifty different cities around this country to be a part of a Resource Seminar for Youth Workers, sponsored by Youth Specialties of El Cajon, California. Each year, we try to give some good practical counsel about how to survive and thrive in youth ministry. As a part of a recent seminar, we gave two principles that bear repeating in this last chapter.

1. *Just do it . . . but don't try to do it all.*

One of the biggest mistakes you could make in reading a book like this is to decide that within the next two weeks, you will implement every good suggestion and new idea that you've gleaned from these chapters. So many times we go to a workshop, or to a convention, or we read some new book, and our natural tendency is to make immediate changes and implement all the new ideas right away.

Sometimes the best approach, before we do anything, is to stop, think through, and pray about some of the ideas. Give yourself some time to incubate these new ideas before you rush out and hatch something prematurely. Perhaps after thinking through some of this material, it would be wise to first implement those ideas and strategies that will cause the least change in the normal program and schedule. Start with those ideas, and then, as leaders and students have time to adjust to those changes, you can implement more.

2. *Something is better than nothing.*

When you read a book like this, you may get depressed. Before reading the book, after all, you thought you were doing pretty well. Now you know all the things you're not doing.

Before you close this book and walk away feeling, "My ministry is so weak; we're not doing half of this stuff," remember that something is better than nothing. If you have one student involved in Bible study, that is better than nothing. If you have motivated one student to more completely serve and obey God, that is better than nothing. It is the Enemy who constantly accuses us of our shortcomings and our shortfalls. God does not call us to multiply our talents tenfold. He only asks that we use the gifts we have to invest in the kingdom.

THE BUILDING CODE

Does that mean then that we can sit back and wait for God to "do it" without too much concern about depth and style in our programs? By no means.

The fun part of youth ministry is getting new kids to come out, and helping students, maybe for the first time, to discover the love and power of Jesus. I have been privileged to be a part of that enterprise now for almost two decades. There is no question that sometimes the excitement of that ministry is overshadowed by the tedious, ongoing work of discipling and helping students to learn how to obey God.

But when our adolescent Elishas move away from us, and cross the river, it will be that kind of day-to-day nurture that stands them in good stead.

For that reason, Paul's own ministry of nurture adhered to a strict building code that he took very seriously. May it be our caution and our calling as we close this book and go out to our own ministries of nurture.

Each one should be careful how he builds. For no one can lay any foundation other than the one already laid, which is Jesus Christ. If any man builds on this foundation using gold, silver, costly stones, wood, hay or straw, his work will be shown for what it is, because the Day will bring it to light. It will be revealed with fire, and the fire will test the quality of each man's work" (1 Corinthians 3:10–13).